CHUANG TZU

Translations from the Asian Classics

Translations from the Asian Classics

Editorial Board

CHUANG TZU

 BASIC WRITINGS

Translated by BURTON WATSON

New York

COLUMBIA UNIVERSITY PRESS

Library of Congress Catalog Card Number: 64-21079
ISBN 0-231-08606-7   ISBN 0-231-10595-9 (pbk.)
Printed in the United States of America

40 39 38 37 36 35 34 33 32 31

CONTENTS

PREFACE

In 815 the Chinese poet-official Po Chü-i, having offended the authorities by his outspoken criticisms of government policy, was dismissed from his position at court and shunted off to an insignificant post in the Yangtze region far to the south, a virtual sentence of exile. Not long after arriving at his new post, he wrote the following poem entitled "Reading Chuang Tzu":

Leaving homeland, parted from kin, banished to a strange place,
I wonder my heart feels so little anguish and pain.
Consulting Chuang Tzu, I find where I belong:
surely my home is there in Not-Even-Anything land.

As a result of his sudden reversal of fortune, Po was abruptly separated from almost everything that defined life for a Chinese gentleman of his class: native region, extended family (his wife was allowed to accompany him into exile), public office. In terms of traditional values, he had in effect been stripped of his identity, his reason for being. One would expect him to be totally crushed by such a turn of events. And yet, to his own surprise, as he declares in the poem, he finds himself relatively untroubled by grief or depression. His reading of Chuang Tzu has enabled him to view himself and his age from a loftier plane, one that transcends conventional concepts of time and place, duty and social position. Chuang Tzu's writings have freed him, as they have so many readers down through the centuries, from his narrower identity as a native of a particular locale, a player in a particular role in life, and made him a dweller in all time and place, in the land that Chuang Tzu calls "Not-Even-Anything" because it is in fact everything and everywhere.

It is no doubt this loftiness and liberality of outlook that has made the work known as the *Chuang Tzu* such an enduring favorite with readers in China and the other countries within the Chinese cultural sphere in the two thousand and more years since its appearance. And it is this same breadth of vision, along with the brilliant and imaginative language in which it is couched, that allows the work to soar over the barriers of translation and win new readers in other countries and cultural spheres. The *Chuang Tzu*'s engaging anecdotes, with their potent wit and humor to propel them, have by now traveled far beyond the borders of Asia, and there are probably few places in the world where the tale of Chuang Tzu's butterfly dream is not known.

Of the four philosophers that I translated in my *Basic Writings* series, the other three, Mo Tzu, Hsün Tzu, and Han Fei Tzu, though they deal with political and moral questions of universal significance, strike one as inseparably linked to ancient China, the age and society that gave them birth. But Chuang Tzu, because of his inspired and unconventional language and the visionary ideas he expounds, seems to float free of his environment and to be in the end addressing all persons and ages. He was, I must admit, the most difficult to translate, but at the same time the most rewarding, because I felt that I was dealing here with a text of timeless import.

In terms of readership as well, I am happy to note, Chuang Tzu appears to be in an orbit of his own. While the other philosophers in the *Basic Writings* series have steady but quite modest annual sales, presumably mainly to students who are taking courses in Asian thought or culture, Chuang Tzu seems to have been able to reach out to a much broader and more varied audience. It is to be hoped that in this newly revised edition, he will continue to expand his circle of readers, further testimony to the lasting appeal and importance of his writings.

OUTLINE OF EARLY CHINESE HISTORY

(Dates and entries before 841 B.C. are traditional)

B.C.	Dynasty		
2852		Culture Heroes	Fu Hsi, inventor of writing, fishing, trapping.
2737			Shen Nung, inventor of agriculture, commerce.
2697			Yellow Emperor.
2357		Sage Kings	Yao.
2255			Shun.
2205			Yü, virtuous founder of dynasty.
1818	Hsia Dynasty		Chieh, degenerate terminator of dynasty.
1766	Shang or Yin Dynasty		King T'ang, virtuous founder of dynasty.
[c. 1300]			[Beginning of archeological evidence.]
1154			Chou, degenerate terminator of dynasty.

Date	Dynasty	Period	Event
	Three Dynasties		King Wen, virtuous founder of dynasty.
1122			King Wu, virtuous founder of dynasty.
1115	Chou Dynasty	Western Chou	King Ch'eng, virtuous founder of dynasty.
			(Duke of Chou, regent to King Ch'eng)
878			King Li.
781			
771			King Yu.
722			
		Eastern Chou	Spring and Autumn period (722–481).
551			Period of the "hundred philosophers" (551–c. 233): Confucius, Mo Tzu, Lao Tzu (?), Mencius, Chuang Tzu, Hui Shih, Shang Yang, Kung-sun Lung, Hsün Tzu, Han Fei Tzu.
403			Warring States period (403–221).
4th to 3d cent.			Extensive wall-building and waterworks by Ch'in and other states.
249			Lü Pu-wei, prime minister of Ch'in.
221	Ch'in Dynasty (221–207 B.C.)		The First Emperor; Li Ssu, prime minister.
214			The Great Wall completed.

CHUANG TZU

INTRODUCTION

All we know about the identity of Chuang Tzu, or Master Chuang, are the few facts recorded in the brief notice given him in the *Shih chi* or *Records of the Historian* (ch. 63) by Ssu-ma Ch'ien (145?–89? B.C.). According to this account, his personal name was Chou, he was a native of a place called Meng, and he once served as "an official in the lacquer garden" in Meng. Ssu-ma Ch'ien adds that he lived at the same time as King Hui (370–319 B.C.) of Liang and King Hsüan (319–301 B.C.) of Ch'i, which would make him a contemporary of Mencius, and that he wrote a work in 100,000 words or more which was "mostly in the nature of fable." A certain number of anecdotes concerning Chuang Tzu appear in the book that bears his name, though it is difficult, in view of the deliberate fantasy that characterizes the book as a whole, to regard these as reliable biography.

Scholars disagree as to whether "lacquer garden" is the name of a specific location, or simply means lacquer groves in general, and the location of Meng is uncertain, though it was probably in present-day Honan, south of the Yellow River. If this last supposition is correct, it means that Chuang Chou was a native of the state of Sung, a fact which may have important implications.

When the Chou people of western China conquered and replaced the Shang or Yin dynasty around the eleventh century B.C., they enfeoffed the descendants of the Shang kings as rulers of the region of Sung in eastern Honan, in order that they might carry on the sacrifices to their illustrious ancestors. Though Sung was never an important state, it managed to maintain its existence throughout the long centuries of the Chou dynasty until 286 B.C., when it was overthrown by three of its neighbors and its territory divided up among them. It is natural to suppose that not only the ruling house, but many of the citizens of Sung as well, were descended from the Shang people, and that they preserved to some extent the rites, customs, and ways of thought that had been characteristic of Shang culture. The *Book of Odes,* it may be noted, contains five "Hymns of Shang" which deal with the legends of the Shang royal family and which scholars agree were either composed or handed down by the rulers of the state of Sung. Sung led a precarious existence, constantly invaded or threatened by more powerful neighbors, and in later centuries its weakness was greatly aggravated by incessant internal strife, the ruling house of Sung possessing a history unrivaled for its bloodiness even in an age of disorder. Its inhabitants, as descendants of the conquered Shang people, were undoubtedly despised and oppressed by the more powerful states which belonged to the lineage of the Chou conquerors, and the "man of Sung" appears in the literature of late Chou times as a stock figure of the ignorant simpleton.

All these facts of Sung life—the preservation of the legends and religious beliefs of the Shang people, the political and social oppression, the despair born of weakness and strife—may go far to elucidate the background from which Chuang Tzu's thought sprang, and to explain why, in its skepticism and mystical detachment, it differs so radically from Confucianism, the basically optimistic and strongly political-minded philosophy which developed in the Chou lineage states of Lu and Ch'i. But since we know so little about the life and identity of Chuang Chou or his connection with the book that bears his name, it is perhaps best not to seek too assiduously to establish a direct causal connection between the background and the philosophy.

Whoever Chuang Chou was, the writings attributed to him bear the stamp of a brilliant and original mind. Instead of speculating upon the possible sources from which this mind drew its ideas, let us turn to an examination of the ideas themselves. I shall simply state that from here on, when I speak of Chuang Tzu, I am referring not to a specific individual known to us through history, but to the mind, or group of minds, revealed in the text called *Chuang Tzu*, particularly the first seven sections of that text.

The central theme of the *Chuang Tzu* may be summed up in a single word: freedom. Essentially, all the philosophers of ancient China addressed themselves to the same problem: how is man to live in a world dominated by chaos, suffering, and absurdity? Nearly all of them answered with some concrete plan of action designed to reform the individual, to reform society, and eventually to free the world from its ills. The proposals put forward by the Confucians, the Mo-ists, and the Legalists, to name some of the principal schools of philosophy, are all different, but all are based upon the same kind of common-sense approach to the problem, and all seek for concrete social, political, and ethical reforms to solve it. Chuang Tzu's answer, however, the answer of one branch of the Taoist school, is radically different from these, and is grounded upon a wholly different type of thinking. It is the answer of a mystic, and in attempting to describe it here in clear and concrete language, I shall undoubtedly be doing violence to its essentially mystic and indescribable nature. Chuang Tzu's answer to the question is: free yourself from the world.

What does he mean by this? In a section not translated here (sec. 23), he tells the story of a man named Nan-jung Chu who went to visit the Taoist sage Lao Tzu in hopes of finding some solution to his worries. When he appeared, Lao Tzu promptly inquired, "Why did you come with all this crowd of people?" The man whirled around in astonishment to see if there was someone standing behind him. Needless to say, there was not; the "crowd of people" that he came with was the baggage of old ideas, the conventional concepts of right and wrong, good and bad, life and death, that he lugged about with him wherever he went.

It is this baggage of conventional values that man must first of all discard before he can be free. Chuang Tzu saw the same human sufferings that Confucius, Mo Tzu, and Mencius saw. He saw the man-made ills of war, poverty, and injustice. He saw the natural ills of disease and death. But he believed that they were ills only because man recognized them as such. If man would once forsake his habit of labeling things good or bad, desirable or undesirable, then the man-made ills, which are the product of man's purposeful and value-ridden actions, would disappear and the natural ills that remain would no longer be seen as ills, but as an inevitable part of the course of life. Thus, in Chuang Tzu's eyes, man is the author of his own suffering and bondage, and all his fears spring from the web of values created by himself alone. Chuang Tzu sums up this whole diseased, fear-struck condition of mankind in the macabre metaphor of the leper woman who, "when she gives birth to a child in the deep of the night, rushes to fetch a torch and examine it, trembling with terror lest it look like herself" (sec. 12).

But how is one to persuade the leper woman that disease and ugliness are mere labels that have no real validity? It is no easy task, and for this reason the philosophy of Chuang Tzu, like most mystical philosophies, has seldom been fully understood and embraced in its pure form by more than a small minority. Most of the philosophies of ancient China are addressed to the political or intellectual elite; Chuang Tzu's is addressed to the spiritual elite.

Difficult though the task may be, however, Chuang Tzu employs every resource of rhetoric in his efforts to awaken the reader to the essential meaninglessness of conventional values and to free him from their bondage. One device he uses to great effect is the pointed or paradoxical anecdote, the *non sequitur* or apparently nonsensical remark that jolts the mind into awareness of a truth outside the pale of ordinary logic— a device familiar to Western readers of Chinese and Japanese Zen literature. The other device most common in his writings is the pseudological discussion or debate that starts out sounding completely rational and sober, and ends by reducing language to a gibbering inanity. These two devices will be found in their purest form in the first two sections of the *Chuang Tzu*, which together constitute one of the fiercest and most dazzling assaults ever made not only upon man's conventional system of values, but upon his conventional concepts of time, space, reality, and causation as well.

Finally, Chuang Tzu uses throughout his writings that deadliest of weapons against all that is pompous, staid, and holy: humor. Most Chinese philosophers employ humor sparingly—a wise decision, no doubt, in view of the serious tone they seek to maintain—and some of them seem never to have heard of it at all. Chuang Tzu, on the contrary, makes it the very core of his style, for he appears to have known that one good laugh would do more than ten pages of harangue to shake the reader's confidence in the validity of his pat assumptions.

In Chuang Tzu's view, the man who has freed himself from conventional standards of judgment can no longer be made to suffer, for he refuses to recognize poverty as any less desirable than affluence, to recognize death as any less desirable than life. He does not in any literal sense withdraw and hide from the world—to do so would show that he still passed judgment upon the world. He remains within society but refrains from acting out of the motives that lead ordinary men to struggle for wealth, fame, success, or safety. He maintains a state that Chuang Tzu refers to as *wu-wei*, or inaction, meaning by this term not a forced quietude, but a course of action that is not founded upon any purposeful motives of gain or striving. In such a state, all human actions become as spontaneous and mindless as those of the natural world. Man becomes one with Nature, or Heaven, as Chuang Tzu calls it, and merges himself with Tao, or the Way, the underlying unity that embraces man, Nature, and all that is in the universe.

To describe this mindless, purposeless mode of life, Chuang Tzu turns most often to the analogy of the artist or craftsman. The skilled woodcarver, the skilled butcher, the skilled swimmer does not ponder or ratiocinate on the course of action he should take; his skill has become so much a part of him that he merely acts instinctively and spontaneously and, without knowing why, achieves success. Again, Chuang Tzu employs the metaphor of a totally free and purposeless journey, using the word *yu* (to wander, or a wandering) to designate the way in which the enlightened man wanders through all of creation, enjoying its delights without ever becoming attached to any one part of it.

But, like all mystics, Chuang Tzu insists that language is in the end grievously inadequate to describe the true Way, or the wonderful freedom of the man who has realized his identity with it. Again and again, he cautions that he is giving only a "rough" or "reckless" description of these things, and what follows is usually a passage of highly poetic and paradoxical language that in fact conveys little more than the essential ineffability of such a state of being.

These mystical passages, with their wild and whirling words, need not puzzle the reader if he recognizes them for what they are, but there is one aspect of them that calls for comment. Often Chuang Tzu describes the Taoist sage or enlightened man in terms which suggest that he possesses magical powers, that he moves in a trancelike state, that he is impervious to all harm and perhaps even immortal. In these descriptions, Chuang Tzu is probably drawing upon the language of ancient Chinese religion and magic, and there were undoubtedly men in his day, as there were in later centuries, who believed that such magical powers, including the power to become immortal, were attainable. I am inclined to believe that Chuang Tzu— that is, the author of the most profound and penetrating portions of the book which bears his name—intended these descriptions to be taken metaphorically. But there is evidence elsewhere in the *Chuang Tzu* that they were taken literally, and countless followers of the Taoist school in later ages certainly interpreted them that way. Perhaps, as Arthur Waley says, the best approach is not to attempt to draw any sharp line between rationalism and superstition, between philosophy and magic, but to be prepared to find them mingled and overlapping. After all, it is the drawing of forced and unnatural distinctions that Chuang Tzu most vehemently condemns. In the end, the best way to approach Chuang Tzu, I believe, is not to attempt to subject his thought to rational and systematic analysis, but to read and reread his words until one has ceased to think of what he is saying and instead has developed an intuitive sense of the mind moving behind the words, and of the world in which it moves.

Chuang Tzu, along with Lao Tzu, or Lao Tan, has long been revered as one of the founders of the Taoist school. Because it was believed that Lao Tzu was a contemporary of Confucius and that he was the author of the book known as the *Lao Tzu* or *Tao-te-ching*, he has been honored as the prime patriarch of the school, and Chuang Tzu as a later disciple and continuer of his doctrines. Most scholars now agree that it is impossible to say whether Lao Tzu ever lived or, if he did, to determine exactly when. He appears in the pages of the *Chuang Tzu* as one of a number of Taoist sages, but this signifies very little, since so many of the figures in Chuang Tzu's writings are clearly fictitious. Chuang Tzu at no point makes any reference to the *Tao-te-ching;* there are a few places where he uses language that is similar to or identical with that of the *Tao-te-ching,* but these do not prove that one text is earlier than the other, or that there is any direct connection between them. Moreover, Chuang Tzu's brand of Taoism, as often pointed out, is in many respects quite different from that expounded in the *Tao-te-ching.* Therefore, though the two may have drawn upon common sources, and certainly became fused in later times, it seems best to consider them separately— which is why I have not discussed the philosophy of the *Tao-te-ching* here. There is much disagreement among scholars as to when the *Tao-te-ching* attained its present form, though it is safe to assume, I believe, that both the *Chuang Tzu* and the *Tao-te-ching* circulated in something like their present form from the second century B.C. on, that is, from the beginning of the Han dynasty (202 B.C.–A.D. 220).

In the early years of the Han dynasty, the *Tao-te-ching,*

probably because of its brevity and relative simplicity of language, seems to have enjoyed greater popularity than the *Chuang Tzu.* It is repeatedly quoted or alluded to in the literature of the period, and several influential statesmen of the time, including a strong-willed empress dowager, advocated its doctrines. The court official Ssu-ma T'an (d. 110 B.C.), father of the historian Ssu-ma Ch'ien, wrote a brief essay, "A Discussion of the Essentials of the Six Schools," in which he reviewed the doctrines of the most important philosophical schools of the time and came out strongly in favor of Taoism. The *Huai-nan Tzu,* an eclectic work compiled by scholars of the court of Liu An (d. 122 B.C.), the king of Huai-nan, dates from the same period; it includes many excerpts from the *Chuang Tzu* and *Lao Tzu* and, like Ssu-ma T'an, reserves the highest praise for the teachings of the Taoist school.

In spite of this relative popularity, however, Taoism was gradually overshadowed by Confucianism, which won official recognition from the Han emperor toward the end of the second century B.C. and was declared the orthodox philosophy of the state, with a government university set up in the capital to teach its doctrines to prospective officials. This did not mean that Taoist writings were in any way suppressed. People were still free to read and study them, and we may be sure that educated men of the Han continued to savor the literary genius of Chuang Tzu and Lao Tzu as they had in the past. It simply meant that Taoist writings were not accorded any official recognition as the basis for decisions on state and public affairs.

In the intellectual world of late Chou times, a number of rival doctrines had contended for supremacy, and the thinkers of the age had frequently attacked each other with vigor and asperity. Mo Tzu had denounced Confucianism, Mencius and

Hsün Tzu had denounced Mo-ism, and the Legalist philosopher Han Fei Tzu had denounced both doctrines. Chuang Tzu had spent a certain amount of time attacking the philosophers of other schools—the pompously moralistic Confucians and Mo-ists, the Logicians Hui Shih and Kung-sun Lung with their hairsplitting semantics—though his customary weapon was parody and ridicule rather than polemic.

But by the first century B.C., many of the old sharp differences of opinion had been forgotten or softened by time. Moism and the School of Logic had all but disappeared from the intellectual scene, and the principal battle was between the two rival philosophies of government: Confucianism, nominally the official doctrine of the state, with its emphasis upon moral guidance of the people, and Legalism, which stressed regimentation through stern and detailed laws and held a strong attraction for the totalitarian-minded rulers and statesmen of the time. Taoism, being basically apolitical, remained in the background, to be drawn upon by either side, though in Han times it was more often the Confucian scholars who utilized the Taoist concept of inaction to oppose the state monopolies and other large-scale government enterprises advocated by the Legalist-minded officials.[1]

One should therefore think of Confucianism and Taoism in Han times not as rival systems demanding a choice for one side or the other, but rather as two complementary doctrines, an ethical and political system for the conduct of public and family life, and a mystical philosophy for the spiritual nourish-

---

[1] See, for example, the *Yen-t'ieh-lun*, or *Debates on Salt and Iron*, sec. 57, where the Confucian literati quote Lao Tzu to support their ideal of laissez-faire government. Similarly, they quote or refer to Mo-ist teachings when they wish to emphasize frugality and the need to reduce government expenditures.

ment of the individual, with the metaphysical teachings of the *Book of Changes* acting as a bridge between the two.

This approach is well exemplified in the lives of two scholars, Shu Kuang and his nephew Shu Shou, students of the Confucian Classics who served as tutors to the heir apparent of Emperor Hsüan (r. 74–49 B.C.), instructing him in the *Analects* and the *Classic of Filial Piety*. When Shu Kuang felt he had reached the pinnacle of success and honor, he announced, in the words of Lao Tzu, that "he who knows what is enough will not be shamed; he who knows where to stop will not be in danger." He and his nephew then petitioned the emperor for release from their official duties and, when it had been granted, retired to the country. (*Han shu* 71.)

Or, to turn from officialdom to the world of private citizens, we may note the case of a scholar named Yen Chün-p'ing of the region of Szechwan, who made his living as a diviner in the market place of Ch'eng-tu. He admitted that this was a rather lowly occupation, but explained that he pursued it "because I can thereby benefit the common people. When men come to me with questions about something that is evil or improper, I use the oracle as an excuse to advise them on what is right. I advise sons to be filial, younger brothers to be obedient, subjects to be loyal, utilizing whatever the circumstances may be to lead the people to what is right—and over half of them follow my advice!" So Yen Chün-p'ing spent his days instructing the people, in this ingenious fashion, in the dictates of conventional morality. But when he had made enough money for one day, "he shut up his stall, lowered the blinds, and gave instruction in the *Lao Tzu*" (*Han shu* 72). He was the author of a work, which was based on the doctrines of Lao Tzu and Chuang Tzu, and was a teacher of the most eminent

Confucian philosopher of the time, Yang Hsiung (53 B.C.–A.D. 18).

Thus, like so many Chinese of later centuries, these men of the Han were both Confucians and Taoists by turns, depending upon which doctrine was appropriate to their particular activities or phase of life, and in this way they contrived, with considerable success, to enjoy the best of two superb philosophies.

Confucianism continued to receive official support and to dominate the intellectual life of China during the remaining centuries of the Han dynasty. With the decay and final collapse of the dynasty in A.D. 220, the empire split into three rival kingdoms and entered upon an era of strife and disunion, aggravated by repeated foreign invasion, that was to last until the Sui once more unified China in A.D. 581. Though Taoism had by no means been forgotten during the long years of the Han, the shock occasioned by the downfall of the dynasty and the political disorder which ensued led men to reexamine the texts of Taoism and the other ancient schools of philosophy with fresh interest to see if their teachings could be used in some way to supplement or correct the tenets of Confucianism, which had to some extent been discredited or called into doubt by the fall of the dynasty that had espoused them. The gradual spread of Buddhism during these same centuries helped to foster this revival of interest in Taoism, often referred to as Neo-Taoism, because so many of the doctrines of the Indian religion appeared, on the surface at least, to be strikingly similar to those of Lao Tzu and Chuang Tzu.

At this time the philosophy of Chuang Tzu came to be studied and appreciated to a degree unknown before. Its unconventionality and skepticism appealed to an age of disorder in which conventional moral standards seemed to have lost all

validity; its implications of a spiritual elite who could transcend the bonds of the world and wander in a realm beyond
life and death—whether such release was interpreted metaphorically or literally—appealed to a society dominated by aris-
tocratic tastes. It was an age of ferment, of widening intellectual horizons, in many ways like that of Chuang Tzu himself, and one in which Chuang Tzu's mystic vision of freedom
seemed to make better sense than it ever had during the staid
and stable years of the Han empire.

Our present version of the *Chuang Tzu* dates from this period and was edited by Kuo Hsiang (d. A.D. 312), one of the
leaders of the Neo-Taoist movement. Kuo Hsiang appended a
commentary to the text, the oldest commentary now in existence, which may in part be the work of a predecessor, Hsiang
Hsiu, who lived in the first half of the third century A.D. In
any event, it is the text and commentary of Kuo Hsiang's edition of the *Chuang Tzu* that form the basis for all our present
versions of the work.

The bibliography compiled at the end of the first century
B.C. and preserved in the "Treatise on Literature" of the *Han
shu* lists a *Chuang Tzu* in 52 sections. When Kuo Hsiang
compiled his edition some three centuries later, he discarded
a number of sections which he considered to be inferior and
of patently spurious nature, and settled upon a text consisting
of 33 sections. These he divided into three groups in the following order: seven sections called *nei-p'ien,* or "inner chapters," 15 sections called *wai-p'ien,* or "outer chapters," and 11
sections called *tsa-p'ien,* or "miscellaneous chapters." The titles
of the "inner chapters" are descriptive of the theme of the
chapter as a whole, and were probably affixed by the writer
himself. Those of the "outer" and "miscellaneous" chapters,
on the other hand, are taken from the opening words of the

chapter and often have little to do with the chapter as a whole, suggesting that they were added later and that these chapters are in some cases more in the nature of collections of fragments.

It is generally agreed that the seven "inner chapters," all of which are translated here, constitute the heart of the *Chuang Tzu*. They contain all the important ideas, are written in a brilliant and distinctive—though difficult—style, and are probably the earliest in date, though so far no way has been found to prove this last assumption. Whether they are the work of the man called Chuang Chou we do not know, but they are certainly in the main the product of a superbly keen and original mind, though they may contain brief interpolations by other hands. The remainder of the *Chuang Tzu* is a mixture, sections of which may be as old—they are at times almost as brilliant—as the "inner chapters," sections of which may date from as late as the third or fourth centuries A.D. Though they contain many interesting anecdotes and passages of discussion which serve to expand and illustrate the ideas of the "inner chapters," they add little to the philosophy of the *Chuang Tzu* as a whole, and what they do add is often suspiciously foreign to the spirit of the "inner chapters."

Waley, in his discussion of the authorship of the *Chuang Tzu*, states that "some parts are by a splendid poet, others are by a feeble scribbler" (*Three Ways of Thought in Ancient China*, p. 256). Anyone who reads the original with any sensitivity to style will, I believe, readily agree with this observation; parts of the book are as humdrum and repetitious as others are inspired. In making my own selection, I have naturally tried to avoid the feeble scribbler at all cost. This is not always easy to do in the latter sections of the *Chuang Tzu*, however, because the scribbler and the poet are occasionally to be found side by side within a single chapter. I have translated three sections from the "outer chapters" that seem to me to be of particular interest, and one section from the "miscellaneous chapters," making a total of 11 sections. A few other sections that I would like to have included are so marred by textual corruption that I did not feel confident enough to undertake a translation (and textual uncertainties present a serious problem even in the sections I have translated, as is pointed out in my notes).

Though a considerable amount of critical work has been done on the text of the *Chuang Tzu*, and there is an almost endless number of commentaries, the meaning of many passages remains a matter of doubt. There are two reasons for this: the intrinsic difficulty of Chuang Tzu's language and thought, and the textual corruption that has arisen, almost inevitably, we may suppose, in the course of the transmission of such a difficult text.

Chuang Tzu, as I have said, rejects all conventional values, and as a result, like so many mystical writers, he rejects the conventional values of words as well, deliberately employing them to mean the opposite of what they ordinarily mean in order to demonstrate their essential meaninglessness. When a writer does this, he of course invites misunderstanding, no matter how dazzling the literary effect he achieves. This is what has happened to Chuang Tzu. His grammar is regular enough; his sentence patterns are for the most part like those of other writers of the period; but, because what he says is so often the direct opposite of what anyone else would say, commentators have again and again been led to wonder if he really does not mean something other than what he says, or if the text is perhaps corrupt.

To give an example, in order to pry men loose from their

conventional concepts of goodness and beauty, Chuang Tzu deliberately glorifies everything that to ordinary eyes appears sordid, base, or bizarre—ex-criminals who have suffered mutilating punishments, men who are horribly ugly or deformed, creatures of grotesque shape or size. To illustrate the point— and because the passage is so important in Taoist philosophy— let me quote one of Chuang Tzu's most famous descriptions of the Tao or the Way:

Master Tung-kuo asked Chuang Tzu, "This thing called the Way—where does it exist?"

Chuang Tzu said, "There's no place it doesn't exist."

"Come," said Master Tung-kuo, "you must be more specific!"

"It is in the ant."

"As low a thing as that?"

"It is in the panic grass."

"But that's lower still!"

"It is in the tiles and shards."

"How can it be so low?"

"It is in the piss and shit." (sec. 22)

But if, in Chuang Tzu's language, ugly stands for beautiful, or something beyond both beauty and ugliness, and bad stands for good, or something beyond it, then what do beautiful and good stand for? In other words, since Chuang Tzu deliberately turns the values of words upside down, how are we ever to know for certain when he is sincerely praising something? This is the most serious problem one encounters in the interpretation of Taoist writings, as it is in the interpretation of the writings of Zen Buddhism. In any given passage, is the writer, regardless of what words he uses, describing a state of affairs that is in his eyes commendable or uncommendable? Depending upon how one answers this question, the interpretation of the entire passage will differ radically. (An example of this problem is pointed out in note 4 to section 3.)

In translating the other philosophers in this series, I have allowed myself considerable freedom, because I was reasonably confident that I understood what they were saying, and because the exact wording of the original did not seem to be of such vital importance. I have proceeded differently in the case of Chuang Tzu. Chuang Tzu, as has often been pointed out, though he writes in prose, uses words in the manner of a poet, particularly in the lyrical descriptions of the Way or the Taoist sage. In the broader sense of the word, his work is in fact one of the greatest poems of ancient China. For this reason it seems to me particularly important to stick just as closely as possible to the precise wording and imagery of the Chinese. For example, in section 5 there is a passage in which Confucius is pictured discussing the need to harmonize with and delight in all the manifold ups and downs of human existence, to "master them and never be at a loss for joy," adding that one should "make it be spring with everything." This last phrase, literally, "with things make spring," is an example of the highly poetic language which Chuang Tzu employs in such passages, and for which he is justly admired. To render the phrase as "live in peace with mankind" (Giles), or "be kind with things" (Yu-lan Fung), not only blurs the image of the original beyond recognition, but suggests that Chuang Tzu is mouthing clichés when in fact he is using the Chinese language as it has never been used before. No other text of early times, with the possible exception of the *Tso chuan,* so fully exploits the beauties of ancient Chinese—its vigor, its economy, its richness and symmetry—and it is for this reason that I have chosen to render the wording of the original as closely as possible, even though the English which results may at times sound somewhat strange. Chuang Tzu uses words in unconventional ways and he deserves a translation that at least attempts to do justice to his imaginativeness. I have not hesitated to make free use of colloquialisms—a great part of the *Chuang Tzu* is in the form of informal dialogues—or of slang; I do so, however, not in order to create a "jazzy" effect, but because such words or constructions seem to me to get closer to the original than more formal English could. Wherever I have substantially added to the wording of the original in translation, I have enclosed the added words in brackets.

Needless to say, I could not render the literal meaning of the original until I had first decided what it was, and in this sense my translation is as much an interpretation, and as tentative in many places, as any other. In the note on bibliography at the end of this introduction, I have mentioned briefly the commentaries and translations that I have drawn upon. But the result inevitably represents my own interpretation of the text, and will not be quite like that of anyone else. With a work of such difficulty, there can never be anything like a definitive translation, because there is no such thing as a definitive interpretation. Every translator who takes up the text will produce his own *Chuang Tzu,* and the more that are available for the reader to enjoy and compare, the better.

Much of the *Chuang Tzu* consists of anecdotes, often two or three anecdotes in a row that illustrate the same general theme and appear to be hardly more than different versions of a single story. In these anecdotes a variety of historical and semihistorical personages appear, as well as a delightful assortment of gods, mythical heroes, and talking trees, birds, insects, and other creatures. One such historical figure, the logical philosopher Hui Shih or Hui Tzu, who seems to have been a friend of Chuang Tzu, always represents the same viewpoint: that of "intellectuality as opposed to imagination," as Waley puts it (*Three Ways of Thought,* p. 12). But there is no consistency in the variety of viewpoints which the other figures are made to expound. Thus Confucius sometimes preaches conventional Confucian morality, while at other times he speaks in the words of a true Taoist sage, and even Chuang Tzu himself appears on occasion in the role of the convention-ridden fool. The reader must learn to expect any opinion whatsoever from any source, to savor the outrageous incongruities, and to judge for himself which of the opinions offered represents the highest level of enlightenment.

In closing, I may add a word on the translation of certain key philosophical terms in the *Chuang Tzu.* The term *Tao* I have translated throughout as "the Way," in order to remain consistent with the practice adopted in the other translations in this series. It is perfectly true that Chuang Tzu means by this word something quite different from what Mo Tzu, Hsün Tzu, or Han Fei Tzu meant. But all of them used the same Chinese word, and the reader may easily judge for himself how they interpreted it by observing the ways in which they used it. For the same reason, I have rendered *T'ien* as "Heaven," or "heavenly" in nearly all cases. Chuang Tzu uses the word to mean Nature, what pertains to the natural as opposed to the artificial, or as a synonym for the Way. This too is very different from what Mo Tzu or Hsün Tzu meant by the word *T'ien,* but again the reader may judge the differences for himself. In nearly all cases I have rendered *te* as "virtue," except where it has the special meaning of a favor or good deed done for someone. This word presents certain difficulties in Chuang Tzu. Sometimes he employs it to mean conventional virtue—that is, virtue in the Confucian or Mo-ist sense—in which case it has bad connotations; at other times he employs it in a good sense to mean the true virtue or vital power that belongs to the man of Tao. (Compare Waley's rendering of the title *Tao-te-ching* as *The Way and Its Power*.) I prefer not to try to distinguish these two usages in the translation because I do not wish to impose upon the English a distinction that is not explicit in the original. As already mentioned, I render *wu-wei* as "inaction" and *yu* as "to wander" or "wandering." In addition to inventing legendary figures with amusing and often significant names, Chuang Tzu invents a variety of mysterious and high-sounding pseudo-technical terms to refer to the Way or the man who has made himself one with it. I have given a literal translation of such terms, and capitalized them in order to indicate their special character—e.g., Great Clod, Supreme Swindle, True Man. The reader need not puzzle over their precise meaning, since in the end they all refer to essentially the same thing—the inexpressible Absolute.

I have used as the basis of my translation the *Chuang Tzu pu-cheng* of Liu Wen-tien (Shanghai, 1947), principally because of its magnificent legibility, though I have not always followed its punctuation. It would be impractical to list all the commentaries I have drawn upon, directly or indirectly; I have mentioned by name in my notes the commentator I am following in questionable passages, and the reader may identify the works by consulting the exhaustive bibliography of *Chuang Tzu* commentaries in Kuan Feng's translation and study, *Chuang Tzu nei-p'ien i-chieh ho p'i-p'an* (Peking, 1961), pp. 370–403. Two works have been of particular assistance to me: one is the modern language Chinese translation by Kuan Feng cited above; the other is the Japanese translation by Fukunaga

Mitsuji, *Sōshi* (Tokyo, 1956), in the Chūgoku kotensen series. Both translations are confined to the "inner chapters," the first seven sections of the text; but they draw upon all the important recent studies and contain invaluable notes and explanations. No such exhaustive study has as yet been given to the remainder of the *Chuang Tzu* text, and the latter sections of the work contain many unsolved problems. Three important works on the philosophy of Chuang Tzu may be noted here: the *Chuang Tzu hsüeh-an* by Lang Ch'ing-hsiao (Shanghai, 1934; reprinted, Hong Kong, 1963); the *Chuang Tzu che-hsüeh t'ao-lun chi* (Peking, 1962), a collection of essays by Feng Yu-lan, Kuan Feng, and other Chuang Tzu experts; and *Sōshi* (Tokyo, 1964) by Fukunaga Mitsuji, a study of Chuang Tzu's thought. Also of aid to the student and translator of Chuang Tzu is the *Concordance to Chuang Tzu*, Harvard-Yenching Institute Sinological Index Series, Supplement No. 20 (1947).

I have consulted several earlier English translations: that by Herbert A. Giles, *Chuang Tzu: Mystic, Moralist, and Social Reformer* (London, 1889); that by James Legge in *The Sacred Books of the East*, vols. XXXIX–XL; that by Yu-lan Fung (Feng Yu-lan), *Chuang Tzu* (Shanghai, 1933); and the excerpts translated by Arthur Waley in *Three Ways of Thought in Ancient China* (London, 1939), and by Lin Yutang in *The Wisdom of Laotse* (Modern Library, 1948). The first two are complete translations of the *Chuang Tzu;* the third is a translation of the "inner chapters"; while the last two contain excerpts from many different sections. Another complete English translation, by James R. Ware, *The Sayings of Chuang Chou* (New York, New American Library [Mentor] 1963), did not come into my hands until after I had completed my version.

Giles, who produced the first complete English translation,

is very free in his rendering, and again and again substitutes what strike me as tiresome Victorian clichés for the complex and beautiful language of the original. In spite of his offensively "literary" tone, however, he generally gets at what appears to me to be the real meaning of the text. Legge is far more painstaking in reproducing the literal meaning, and for the most part uses a simple, unaffected English that can still be read with pleasure today. But, perhaps because of his long years of work on the Confucian texts, he seems to miss Chuang Tzu's point rather often, and to labor to make common sense out of paradox and fantasy. Yu-lan Fung's work is valuable today mainly because it contains translations from the important Kuo Hsiang commentary. Lin Yutang's *The Wisdom of Laotse* contains a great many well-translated anecdotes and isolated passages from the *Chuang Tzu,* but they have been chopped up and completely rearranged to serve as a commentary on the *Tao-te-ching,* making it very difficult to appreciate the form and relationship which they have in the original. To my mind, by far the most readable and reliable of all Chuang Tzu translations to date are those by Arthur Waley, though unfortunately they represent only a fraction of the text as a whole. I have not had time to examine Professor Ware's translation carefully, though I note that, in his introduction, he describes Chuang Tzu as a member of the "progressive, dynamic wing of Confucianism," which is rather like describing Lucretius as a member of the progressive wing of Stoicism. This strikes me as a flight of fancy that would have astounded even Chuang Tzu, and it is to be hoped that Professor Ware will sometime in the future explain to the world the reasoning upon which it is based.

FREE AND EASY WANDERING

(SECTION I)

In the northern darkness there is a fish and his name is K'un.[1]
The K'un is so huge I don't know how many thousand li he
measures. He changes and becomes a bird whose name is
P'eng. The back of the P'eng measures I don't know how
many thousand li across and, when he rises up and flies off,
his wings are like clouds all over the sky. When the sea begins
to move,[2] this bird sets off for the southern darkness, which
is the Lake of Heaven.

The *Universal Harmony*[3] records various wonders, and it
says: "When the P'eng journeys to the southern darkness,
the waters are roiled for three thousand li. He beats the whirlwind and rises ninety thousand li, setting off on the sixth-
month gale." Wavering heat, bits of dust, living things blown
about by the wind—the sky looks very blue. Is that its real
color, or is it because it is so far away and has no end? When
the bird looks down, all he sees is blue too.

If water is not piled up deep enough, it won't have the
strength to bear up a big boat. Pour a cup of water into a hol-
low in the floor and bits of trash will sail on it like boats. But
set the cup there and it will stick fast, for the water is too

---

[1] *K'un* means fish roe. So Chuang Tzu begins with a paradox—the tiniest
fish imaginable is also the largest fish imaginable.

[2] Probably a reference to some seasonal shift in the tides or currents.

[3] Identified variously as the name of a man or the name of a book. Probably Chuang Tzu intended it as the latter, and is poking fun at the philosophers of other schools who cite ancient texts to prove their assertions.

shallow and the boat too large. If wind is not piled up deep enough, it won't have the strength to bear up great wings. Therefore when the P'eng rises ninety thousand li, he must have the wind under him like that. Only then can he mount on the back of the wind, shoulder the blue sky, and nothing can hinder or block him. Only then can he set his eyes to the south.

The cicada and the little dove laugh at this, saying, "When we make an effort and fly up, we can get as far as the elm or the sapanwood tree, but sometimes we don't make it and just fall down on the ground. Now how is anyone going to go ninety thousand li to the south!"

If you go off to the green woods nearby, you can take along food for three meals and come back with your stomach as full as ever. If you are going a hundred li, you must grind your grain the night before; and if you are going a thousand li, you must start getting the provisions together three months in advance. What do these two creatures understand? Little understanding cannot come up to great understanding; the short-lived cannot come up to the long-lived.

How do I know this is so? The morning mushroom knows nothing of twilight and dawn; the summer cicada knows nothing of spring and autumn. They are the short-lived. South of Ch'u there is a caterpillar which counts five hundred years as one spring and five hundred years as one autumn. Long, long ago there was a great rose of Sharon that counted eight thousand years as one spring and eight thousand years as one autumn. They are the long-lived. Yet P'eng-tsu[4] alone is famous today for having lived a long time, and everybody tries to ape him. Isn't it pitiful!

Among the questions of T'ang to Ch'i we find the same

---

[4] Said to have lived to an incredible old age. See below, p. 78, no. 12.

thing.[5] In the bald and barren north, there is a dark sea, the Lake of Heaven. In it is a fish which is several thousand li across, and no one knows how long. His name is K'un. There is also a bird there, named P'eng, with a back like Mount T'ai and wings like clouds filling the sky. He beats the whirlwind, leaps into the air, and rises up ninety thousand li, cutting through the clouds and mist, shouldering the blue sky, and then he turns his eyes south and prepares to journey to the southern darkness.

The little quail laughs at him, saying, "Where does he think *he's* going? I give a great leap and fly up, but I never get more than ten or twelve yards before I come down fluttering among the weeds and brambles. And that's the best kind of flying anyway! Where does he think *he's* going?" Such is the difference between big and little.

Therefore a man who has wisdom enough to fill one office effectively, good conduct enough to impress one community, virtue enough to please one ruler, or talent enough to be called into service in one state, has the same kind of self-pride as these little creatures. Sung Jung-tzu[6] would certainly burst out laughing at such a man. The whole world could praise Sung Jung-tzu and it wouldn't make him exert himself; the whole world could condemn him and it wouldn't make him mope.

[5] The text may be faulty at this point. The *Pei-shan-lu*, a work written around A.D. 800 by the monk Shen-ch'ing, contains the following passage, said by a T'ang commentator on the *Pei-shan-lu* to be found in the *Chuang Tzu*: "T'ang asked Ch'i, 'Do up, down, and the four directions have a limit?' Ch'i replied, 'Beyond their limitlessness there is still another limitlessness.'" But whether this passage was in the original *Chuang Tzu*, or whether, if it was, it belongs at this point in the text, are questions that cannot be answered.

[6] Referred to elsewhere in the literature of the period as Sung Chien or Sung K'eng. According to the last section of the *Chuang Tzu*, he taught a doctrine of social harmony, frugality, pacifism, and the rejection of conventional standards of honor and disgrace.

He drew a clear line between the internal and the external, and recognized the boundaries of true glory and disgrace. But that was all. As far as the world went, he didn't fret and worry, but there was still ground he left unturned.

Lieh Tzu[7] could ride the wind and go soaring around with cool and breezy skill, but after fifteen days he came back to earth. As far as the search for good fortune went, he didn't fret and worry. He escaped the trouble of walking, but he still had to depend on something to get around. If he had only mounted on the truth of Heaven and Earth, ridden the changes of the six breaths, and thus wandered through the boundless, then what would he have had to depend on? Therefore I say, the Perfect Man has no self; the Holy Man has no merit; the Sage has no fame.[8]

Yao wanted to cede the empire to Hsü Yu. "When the sun and moon have already come out," he said, "it's a waste of light to go on burning the torches, isn't it? When the seasonal rains are falling, it's a waste of water to go on irrigating the fields. If you took the throne, the world would be well ordered. I go on occupying it, but all I can see are my failings. I beg to turn over the world to you."

Hsü Yu said, "You govern the world and the world is already well governed. Now if I take your place, will I be doing it for a name? But name is only the guest of reality—will I be doing it so I can play the part of a guest? When the tailor-bird builds her nest in the deep wood, she uses no more than one branch. When the mole drinks at the river, he takes no more than a bellyful. Go home and forget the matter, my lord.

---

[7] Lieh Yü-k'ou, a Taoist philosopher frequently mentioned in the *Chuang Tzu*. The *Lieh Tzu*, a work attributed to him, is of uncertain date and did not reach its present form until the 3d or 4th centuries A.D.

[8] Not three different categories but three names for the same thing.

I have no use for the rulership of the world! Though the cook may not run his kitchen properly, the priest and the impersonator of the dead at the sacrifice do not leap over the wine casks and sacrificial stands and go take his place." [9]

Chien Wu said to Lien Shu, "I was listening to Chieh Yü's talk—big and nothing to back it up, going on and on without turning around. I was completely dumfounded at his words— no more end than the Milky Way, wild and wide of the mark, never coming near human affairs!"

"What were his words like?" asked Lien Shu.

"He said that there is a Holy Man living on faraway Ku-she Mountain, with skin like ice or snow, and gentle and shy like a young girl. He doesn't eat the five grains, but sucks the wind, drinks the dew, climbs up on the clouds and mist, rides a flying dragon, and wanders beyond the four seas. By concentrating his spirit, he can protect creatures from sickness and plague and make the harvest plentiful. I thought this was all insane and refused to believe it."

"You would!" said Lien Shu. "We can't expect a blind man to appreciate beautiful patterns or a deaf man to listen to bells and drums. And blindness and deafness are not confined to the body alone—the understanding has them too, as your words just now have shown. This man, with this virtue of his, is about to embrace the ten thousand things and roll them into one. Though the age calls for reform, why should he wear himself out over the affairs of the world? There is nothing that can harm this man. Though flood waters pile up to the sky, he will not drown. Though a great drought melts metal and

* Or, following another interpretation, "the priest and the impersonator of the dead do not snatch his wine casks and chopping board away from him and take his place."

stone and scorches the earth and hills, he will not be burned.
From his dust and leavings alone you could mold a Yao or a
Shun! Why should he consent to bother about mere things?"

A man of Sung who sold ceremonial hats made a trip to
Yüeh, but the Yüeh people cut their hair short and tattoo
their bodies and had no use for such things. Yao brought order
to the people of the world and directed the government of all
within the seas. But he went to see the Four Masters of the far
away Ku-she Mountain, [and when he got home] north of the
Fen River, he was dazed and had forgotten his kingdom there.

Hui Tzu[10] said to Chuang Tzu, "The king of Wei gave me
some seeds of a huge gourd. I planted them, and when they
grew up, the fruit was big enough to hold five piculs. I tried
using it for a water container, but it was so heavy I couldn't
lift it. I split it in half to make dippers, but they were so large
and unwieldy that I couldn't dip them into anything. It's not
that the gourds weren't fantastically big—but I decided they
were no use and so I smashed them to pieces."

Chuang Tzu said, "You certainly are dense when it comes
to using big things! In Sung there was a man who was skilled
at making a salve to prevent chapped hands, and generation
after generation his family made a living by bleaching silk in
water. A traveler heard about the salve and offered to buy the
prescription for a hundred measures of gold. The man called
everyone to a family council. 'For generations we've been
bleaching silk and we've never made more than a few measures of gold,' he said. 'Now, if we sell our secret, we can make

---

[10] The logician Hui Shih who, as pointed out by Waley, in the *Chuang
Tzu* "stands for intellectuality as opposed to imagination."

a hundred measures in one morning. Let's let him have it!'
The traveler got the salve and introduced it to the king of Wu,
who was having trouble with the state of Yüeh. The king put
the man in charge of his troops, and that winter they fought
a naval battle with the men of Yüeh and gave them a bad
beating.[11] A portion of the conquered territory was awarded
to the man as a fief. The salve had the power to prevent
chapped hands in either case; but one man used it to get a fief,
while the other one never got beyond silk bleaching—because
they used it in different ways. Now you had a gourd big
enough to hold five piculs. Why didn't you think of making
it into a great tub so you could go floating around the rivers
and lakes, instead of worrying because it was too big and
unwieldy to dip into things! Obviously you still have a lot of
underbrush in your head!"

Hui Tzu said to Chuang Tzu, "I have a big tree called
a *shu*. Its trunk is too gnarled and bumpy to apply a measuring line to, its branches too bent and twisty to match up to
a compass or square. You could stand it by the road and no
carpenter would look at it twice. Your words, too, are big and
useless, and so everyone alike spurns them!"

Chuang Tzu said, "Maybe you've never seen a wildcat or
a weasel. It crouches down and hides, watching for something
to come along. It leaps and races east and west, not hesitating
to go high or low—until it falls into the trap and dies in the
net. Then again there's the yak, big as a cloud covering the
sky. It certainly knows how to be big, though it doesn't know
how to catch rats. Now you have this big tree and you're dis-

[11] Because the salve, by preventing the soldiers' hands from chapping,
made it easier for them to handle their weapons.

tressed because it's useless. Why don't you plant it in Not-Even-Anything Village, or the field of Broad-and-Boundless, relax and do nothing by its side, or lie down for a free and easy sleep under it? Axes will never shorten its life, nothing can ever harm it. If there's no use for it, how can it come to grief or pain?"

# DISCUSSION ON MAKING
ALL THINGS EQUAL

(SECTION 2)

Tzu-ch'i of South Wall sat leaning on his armrest, staring up at the sky and breathing—vacant and far away, as though he'd lost his companion.[1] Yen Ch'eng Tzu-yu, who was standing by his side in attendance, said, "What is this? Can you really make the body like a withered tree and the mind like dead ashes? The man leaning on the armrest now is not the one who leaned on it before!"

Tzu-ch'i said, "You do well to ask the question, Yen. Now I have lost myself. Do you understand that? You hear the piping of men, but you haven't heard the piping of earth. Or if you've heard the piping of earth, you haven't heard the piping of Heaven!"

Tzu-yu said, "May I venture to ask what this means?"

Tzu-ch'i said, "The Great Clod belches out breath and its name is wind. So long as it doesn't come forth, nothing happens. But when it does, then ten thousand hollows begin crying wildly. Can't you hear them, long drawn out? In the mountain forests that lash and sway, there are huge trees a hundred spans around with hollows and openings like noses, like mouths, like ears, like jugs, like cups, like mortars, like rifts, like ruts. They roar like waves, whistle like arrows, screech, gasp, cry, wail, moan, and howl, those in the lead calling out *yeee!*, those behind calling out *yuuu!* In a gentle

---

[1] The word "companion" is interpreted variously to mean his associates, his wife, or his own body.

breeze they answer faintly, but in a full gale the chorus is gigantic. And when the fierce wind has passed on, then all the hollows are empty again. Have you never seen the tossing and trembling that goes on?"

Tzu-yu said, "By the piping of earth, then, you mean simply [the sound of] these hollows, and by the piping of man [the sound of] flutes and whistles. But may I ask about the piping of Heaven?"

Tzu-ch'i said, "Blowing on the ten thousand things in a different way, so that each can be itself—all take what they want for themselves, but who does the sounding?"[2]

Great understanding is broad and unhurried; little understanding is cramped and busy. Great words are clear and limpid;[3] little words are shrill and quarrelsome. In sleep, men's spirits go visiting; in waking hours, their bodies hustle. With everything they meet they become entangled. Day after day they use their minds in strife, sometimes grandiose, sometimes sly, sometimes petty. Their little fears are mean and trembly; their great fears are stunned and overwhelming. They bound off like an arrow or a crossbow pellet, certain that they are the arbiters of right and wrong. They cling to their position as though they had sworn before the gods, sure that they are holding on to victory. They fade like fall and winter—such is the way they dwindle day by day. They drown in what they do— you cannot make them turn back. They grow dark, as though sealed with seals—such are the excesses of their old age. And when their minds draw near to death, nothing can restore them to the light.

Joy, anger, grief, delight, worry, regret, fickleness, inflex-

---

[2] Heaven is not something distinct from earth and man, but a name applied to the natural and spontaneous functioning of the two.

[3] Reading *tan* instead of *yen*.

ibility, modesty, willfulness, candor, insolence—music from empty holes, mushrooms springing up in dampness, day and night replacing each other before us, and no one knows where they sprout from. Let it be! Let it be! [It is enough that] morning and evening we have them, and they are the means by which we live. Without them we would not exist; without us they would have nothing to take hold of. This comes close to the matter. But I do not know what makes them the way they are. It would seem as though they have some True Master, and yet I find no trace of him. He can act—that is certain. Yet I cannot see his form. He has identity but no form.

The hundred joints, the nine openings, the six organs, all come together and exist here [as my body]. But which part should I feel closest to? I should delight in all parts, you say? But there must be one I ought to favor more. If not, are they all of them mere servants? But if they are all servants, then how can they keep order among themselves? Or do they take turns being lord and servant? It would seem as though there must be some True Lord among them. But whether I succeed in discovering his identity or not, it neither adds to nor detracts from his Truth.

Once a man receives this fixed bodily form, he holds on to it, waiting for the end. Sometimes clashing with things, sometimes bending before them, he runs his course like a galloping steed, and nothing can stop him. Is he not pathetic? Sweating and laboring to the end of his days and never seeing his accomplishment, utterly exhausting himself and never knowing where to look for rest—can you help pitying him? I'm not dead yet! he says, but what good is that? His body decays, his mind follows it—can you deny that this is a great sorrow? Man's life has always been a muddle like this. How could I be the only muddled one, and other men not muddled?

If a man follows the mind given him and makes it his teacher, then who can be without a teacher? Why must you comprehend the process of change and form your mind on that basis before you can have a teacher? Even an idiot has his teacher. But to fail to abide by this mind and still insist upon your rights and wrongs—this is like saying that you set off for Yüeh today and got there yesterday.[4] This is to claim that what doesn't exist exists. If you claim that what doesn't exist exists, then even the holy sage Yü couldn't understand you, much less a person like me!

Words are not just wind. Words have something to say. But if what they have to say is not fixed, then do they really say something? Or do they say nothing? People suppose that words are different from the peeps of baby birds, but is there any difference, or isn't there? What does the Way rely upon,[5] that we have true and false? What do words rely upon, that we have right and wrong? How can the Way go away and not exist? How can words exist and not be acceptable? When the Way relies on little accomplishments and words rely on vain show, then we have the rights and wrongs of the Confucians and the Mo-ists. What one calls right the other calls wrong; what one calls wrong the other calls right. But if we want to right their wrongs and wrong their rights, then the best thing to use is clarity.

Everything has its "that," everything has its "this." From the point of view of "that" you cannot see it, but through understanding you can know it. So I say, "that" comes out of "this" and "this" depends on "that"—which is to say that

[4] According to the last section of the *Chuang Tzu*, this was one of the paradoxes of the logician Hui Tzu.

[5] Following the interpretation of Chang Ping-lin. The older interpretation of *yin* here and in the following sentences is, "What is the Way hidden by," etc.

"this" and "that" give birth to each other. But where there is birth there must be death; where there is death there must be birth. Where there is acceptability there must be unacceptability; where there is unacceptability there must be acceptability. Where there is recognition of right there must be recognition of wrong; where there is recognition of wrong there must be recognition of right. Therefore the sage does not proceed in such a way, but illuminates all in the light of Heaven.[6] He too recognizes a "this," but a "this" which is also "that;" a "that" which is also "this." His "that" has both a right and a wrong in it; his "this" too has both a right and a wrong in it. So, in fact, does he still have a "this" and "that"? Or does he in fact no longer have a "this" and "that"? A state in which "this" and "that" no longer find their opposites is called the hinge of the Way. When the hinge is fitted into the socket, it can respond endlessly. Its right then is a single endlessness and its wrong too is a single endlessness. So I say, the best thing to use is clarity.

To use an attribute to show that attributes are not attributes is not as good as using a nonattribute to show that attributes are not attributes. To use a horse to show that a horse is not a horse is not as good as using a non-horse to show that a horse is not a horse,[7] Heaven and earth are one attribute; the ten thousand things are one horse.

What is acceptable we call acceptable; what is unacceptable we call unacceptable. A road is made by people walking on it; things are so because they are called so. What makes them so? Making them so makes them so. What makes them not so?

---

[6] *T'ien*, which for Chuang Tzu means Nature or the Way.

[7] A reference to the statements of the logician Kung-sun Lung, "A white horse is not a horse" and "Attributes are not attributes in and of themselves."

Making them not so makes them not so. Things all must have that which is so; things all must have that which is acceptable. There is nothing that is not so, nothing that is not acceptable.

For this reason, whether you point to a little stalk or a great pillar, a leper or the beautiful Hsi-shih, things ribald and shady or things grotesque and strange, the Way makes them all into one. Their dividedness is their completeness; their completeness is their impairment. No thing is either complete or impaired, but all are made into one again. Only the man of far-reaching vision knows how to make them into one. So he has no use [for categories], but relegates all to the constant. The constant is the useful; the useful is the passable; the passable is the successful; and with success, all is accomplished. He relies upon this alone, relies upon it and does not know he is doing so. This is called the Way.

But to wear out your brain trying to make things into one without realizing that they are all the same—this is called "three in the morning." What do I mean by "three in the morning"? When the monkey trainer was handing out acorns, he said, "You get three in the morning and four at night." This made all the monkeys furious. "Well, then," he said, "you get four in the morning and three at night." The monkeys were all delighted. There was no change in the reality behind the words, and yet the monkeys responded with joy and anger. Let them, if they want to. So the sage harmonizes with both right and wrong and rests in Heaven the Equalizer. This is called walking two roads.

The understanding of the men of ancient times went a long way. How far did it go? To the point where some of them believed that things have never existed—so far, to the end, where nothing can be added. Those at the next stage thought that things exist but recognized no boundaries among them. Those at the next stage thought there were boundaries but recognized no right and wrong. Because right and wrong appeared, the Way was injured, and because the Way was injured, love became complete. But do such things as completion and injury really exist, or do they not?

There is such a thing as completion and injury—Mr. Chao playing the lute is an example. There is such a thing as no completion and no injury—Mr. Chao not playing the lute is an example.[8] Chao Wen played the lute; Music Master K'uang waved his baton; Hui Tzu leaned on his desk. The knowledge of these three was close to perfection. All were masters, and therefore their names have been handed down to later ages. Only in their likes they were different from him [the true sage]. What they liked, they tried to make clear. What he is not clear about, they tried to make clear, and so they ended in the foolishness of "hard" and "white."[9] Their sons, too, devoted all their lives to their fathers'[10] theories, but till their death never reached any completion. Can these men be said to have attained completion? If so, then so have all the rest of us. Or can they not be said to have attained completion? If so, then neither we nor anything else have ever attained it.

The torch of chaos and doubt—this is what the sage steers

[8] Chao Wen was a famous lute (*ch'in*) player. But the best music he could play (i.e., complete) was only a pale and partial reflection of the ideal music, which was thereby injured and impaired, just as the unity of the Way was injured by the appearance of love—i.e., man's likes and dislikes. Hence, when Mr. Chao refrained from playing the lute, there was neither completion nor injury.

[9] The logicians Hui Tzu and Kung-sun Lung spent much time discussing the relationship between attributes such as "hard" and "white" and the thing to which they pertain.

[10] Following Yu-lan Fung and Fukunaga, I read *fu* instead of *wen*.

by.[11] So he does not use things but relegates all to the constant. This is what it means to use clarity.

Now I am going to make a statement here. I don't know whether it fits into the category of other people's statements or not. But whether it fits into their category or whether it doesn't, it obviously fits into some category. So in that respect it is no different from their statements. However, let me try making my statement.

There is a beginning. There is a not yet beginning to be a beginning. There is a not yet beginning to be a not yet beginning to be a beginning. There is being. There is nonbeing. There is a not yet beginning to be nonbeing. There is a not yet beginning to be a not yet beginning to be nonbeing. Suddenly there is being and nonbeing. But between this being and nonbeing, I don't really know which is being and which is nonbeing. Now I have just said something. But I don't know whether what I have said has really said something or whether it hasn't said something.

There is nothing in the world bigger than the tip of an autumn hair, and Mount T'ai is little. No one has lived longer than a dead child, and P'eng-tsu died young.[12] Heaven and earth were born at the same time I was, and the ten thousand things are one with me.

We have already become one, so how can I say anything? But I have just *said* that we are one, so how can I not be saying

[11] He accepts things as they are, though to the ordinary person attempting to establish values they appear chaotic and doubtful and in need of clarification.

[12] The strands of animal fur were believed to grow particularly fine in autumn; hence "the tip of an autumn hair" is a cliché for something extremely tiny. P'eng-tsu, the Chinese Methuselah, has already appeared on p. 24 above.

something? The one and what I said about it make two, and two and the original one make three. If we go on this way, then even the cleverest mathematician can't tell where we'll end, much less an ordinary man. If by moving from nonbeing to being we get to three, how far will we get if we move from being to being? Better not to move, but to let things be!

The Way has never known boundaries; speech has no constancy. But because of [the recognition of a] "this," there came to be boundaries. Let me tell you what the boundaries are. There is left, there is right, there are theories, there are debates,[13] there are divisions, there are discriminations, there are emulations, and there are contentions. These are called the Eight Virtues.[14] As to what is beyond the Six Realms,[15] the sage admits it exists but does not theorize. As to what is within the Six Realms, he theorizes but does not debate. In the case of the *Spring and Autumn*,[16] the record of the former kings of past ages, the sage debates but does not discriminate. So [I say,] those who divide fail to divide; those who discriminate fail to discriminate. What does this mean, you ask? The sage embraces things. Ordinary men discriminate among them and parade their discriminations before others. So I say, those who discriminate fail to see.

The Great Way is not named; Great Discriminations are not spoken; Great Benevolence is not benevolent; Great Modesty

[13] Following the reading in the Ts'ui text.

[14] Many commentators and translators try to give the word *te* some special meaning other than its ordinary one of "virtue" in this context. But I believe Chuang Tzu is deliberately parodying the ethical categories of the Confucians and Mo-ists.

[15] Heaven, earth, and the four directions, i.e., the universe.

[16] Perhaps a reference to the *Spring and Autumn Annals*, a history of the state of Lu said to have been compiled by Confucius. But it may be a generic term referring to the chronicles of the various feudal states.

is not humble; Great Daring does not attack. If the Way is
made clear, it is not the Way. If discriminations are put into
words, they do not suffice. If benevolence has a constant object, it cannot be universal.[17] If modesty is fastidious, it cannot
be trusted. If daring attacks, it cannot be complete. These five
are all round, but they tend toward the square.[18]

Therefore understanding that rests in what it does not understand is the finest. Who can understand discriminations
that are not spoken, the Way that is not a way? If he can
understand this, he may be called the Reservoir of Heaven.
Pour into it and it is never full, dip from it and it never runs
dry, and yet it does not know where the supply comes from.
This is called the Shaded Light.[19]

So it is that long ago Yao said to Shun, "I want to attack the
rulers of Tsung, K'uai, and Hsü-ao. Even as I sit on my throne,
this thought nags at me. Why is this?"

Shun replied, "These three rulers are only little dwellers in
the weeds and brush. Why this nagging desire? Long ago, ten
suns came out all at once and the ten thousand things were
all lighted up. And how much greater is virtue than these
suns!" [20]

Nieh Ch'üeh asked Wang Ni, "Do you know what all
things agree in calling right?"

"How would I know that?" said Wang Ni.

"Do you know that you don't know it?"

"How would I know that?"

"Then do things know nothing?"

[17] Reading *chou* instead of *ch'eng*.

[18] All are originally perfect, but may become "squared," i.e., impaired, by
the misuses mentioned.

[19] Or, according to another interpretation, "the Precious Light."

[20] Here virtue is to be understood in a good sense, as the power of the
Way.

"How would I know that? However, suppose I try saying something. What way do I have of knowing that if I say I know something I don't really not know it? Or what way do I have of knowing that if I say I don't know something I don't really in fact know it? Now let me ask *you* some questions. If a man sleeps in a damp place, his back aches and he ends up half paralyzed, but is this true of a loach? If he lives in a tree, he is terrified and shakes with fright, but is this true of a monkey? Of these three creatures, then, which one knows the proper place to live? Men eat the flesh of grass-fed and grain-fed animals, deer eat grass, centipedes find snakes tasty, and hawks and falcons relish mice. Of these four, which knows how food ought to taste? Monkeys pair with monkeys, deer go out with deer, and fish play around with fish. Men claim that Mao-ch'iang and Lady Li were beautiful, but if fish saw them they would dive to the bottom of the stream, if birds saw them they would fly away, and if deer saw them they would break into a run. Of these four, which knows how to fix the standard of beauty for the world? The way I see it, the rules of benevolence and righteousness and the paths of right and wrong are all hopelessly snarled and jumbled. How could I know anything about such discriminations?"

Nieh Ch'üeh said, "If you don't know what is profitable or harmful, then does the Perfect Man likewise know nothing of such things?"

Wang Ni replied, "The Perfect Man is godlike. Though the great swamps blaze, they cannot burn him; though the great rivers freeze, they cannot chill him; though swift lightning splits the hills and howling gales shake the sea, they cannot frighten him. A man like this rides the clouds and mist, straddles the sun and moon, and wanders beyond the four seas.

Even life and death have no effect on him, much less the rules of profit and loss!"

Chü Ch'üeh-tzu said to Chang Wu-tzu, "I have heard Confucius say that the sage does not work at anything, does not pursue profit, does not dodge harm, does not enjoy being sought after, does not follow the Way, says nothing yet says something, says something yet says nothing, and wanders beyond the dust and grime. Confucius himself regarded these as wild and flippant words, though I believe they describe the working of the mysterious Way. What do you think of them?"

Chang Wu-tzu said, "Even the Yellow Emperor would be confused if he heard such words, so how could you expect Confucius to understand them? What's more, you're too hasty in your own appraisal. You see an egg and demand a crowing cock, see a crossbow pellet and demand a roast dove. I'm going to try speaking some reckless words and I want you to listen to them recklessly. How will that be? The sage leans on the sun and moon, tucks the universe under his arm, merges himself with things, leaves the confusion and muddle as it is, and looks on slaves as exalted. Ordinary men strain and struggle; the sage is stupid and blockish. He takes part in ten thousand ages and achieves simplicity in oneness. For him, all the ten thousand things are what they are, and thus they enfold each other.

"How do I know that loving life is not a delusion? How do I know that in hating death I am not like a man who, having left home in his youth, has forgotten the way back?

"Lady Li was the daughter of the border guard of Ai.[21] When she was first taken captive and brought to the state of

---

[21] She was taken captive by Duke Hsien of Chin in 671 B.C., and later became his consort.

Chin, she wept until her tears drenched the collar of her robe. But later, when she went to live in the palace of the ruler, shared his couch with him, and ate the delicious meats of his table, she wondered why she had ever wept. How do I know that the dead do not wonder why they ever longed for life?

"He who dreams of drinking wine may weep when morning comes; he who dreams of weeping may in the morning go off to hunt. While he is dreaming he does not know it is a dream, and in his dream he may even try to interpret a dream. Only after he wakes does he know it was a dream. And someday there will be a great awakening when we know that this is all a great dream. Yet the stupid believe they are awake, busily and brightly assuming they understand things, calling this man ruler, that one herdsman—how dense! Confucius and you are both dreaming! And when I say you are dreaming, I am dreaming, too. Words like these will be labeled the Supreme Swindle. Yet, after ten thousand generations, a great sage may appear who will know their meaning, and it will still be as though he appeared with astonishing speed.

"Suppose you and I have had an argument. If you have beaten me instead of my beating you, then are you necessarily right and am I necessarily wrong? If I have beaten you instead of your beating me, then am I necessarily right and are you necessarily wrong? Is one of us right and the other wrong? Are both of us right or are both of us wrong? If you and I don't know the answer, then other people are bound to be even more in the dark. Whom shall we get to decide what is right? Shall we get someone who agrees with you to decide? But if he already agrees with you, how can he decide fairly? Shall we get someone who agrees with me? But if he already agrees with me, how can he decide? Shall we get someone who disagrees with both of us? But if he already disagrees with both of us,

how can he decide? Shall we get someone who agrees with
both of us? But if he already agrees with both of us, how can
he decide? Obviously, then, neither you nor I nor anyone else
can know the answer. Shall we wait for still another person?

"But waiting for one shifting voice [to pass judgment on]
another is the same as waiting for none of them.[22] Harmonize
them all with the Heavenly Equality, leave them to their endless changes, and so live out your years. What do I mean by
harmonizing them with the Heavenly Equality? Right is not
right; so is not so. If right were really right, it would differ so
clearly from not right that there would be no need for argument. If so were really so, it would differ so clearly from not so
that there would be no need for argument. Forget the years;
forget distinctions. Leap into the boundless and make it your
home!"

Penumbra said to Shadow, "A little while ago you were
walking and now you're standing still; a little while ago you
were sitting and now you're standing up. Why this lack of
independent action?"

Shadow said, "Do I have to wait for something before I can
be like this? Does what I wait for also have to wait for something before it can be like this? Am I waiting for the scales
of a snake or the wings of a cicada? How do I know why it is
so? How do I know why it isn't so?"[23]

[22] I follow the rearrangement of the text suggested by Lü Hui-ch'ing.
But the text of this whole paragraph leaves much to be desired and the
translation is tentative.

[23] That is, to ordinary men the shadow appears to depend upon something
else for its movement, just as the snake depends on its scales (according to
Chinese belief) and the cicada on its wings. But do such causal views of
action really have any meaning?

Once Chuang Chou dreamt he was a butterfly, a butterfly flitting and fluttering around, happy with himself and doing as he pleased. He didn't know he was Chuang Chou. Suddenly he woke up and there he was, solid and unmistakable Chuang Chou. But he didn't know if he was Chuang Chou who had dreamt he was a butterfly, or a butterfly dreaming he was Chuang Chou. Between Chuang Chou and a butterfly there must be *some* distinction! This is called the Transformation of Things.

THE SECRET OF CARING FOR LIFE[1]

(SECTION 3)

Your life has a limit but knowledge has none. If you use what is limited to pursue what has no limit, you will be in danger. If you understand this and still strive for knowledge, you will be in danger for certain! If you do good, stay away from fame. If you do evil, stay away from punishments. Follow the middle; go by what is constant, and you can stay in one piece, keep yourself alive, look after your parents, and live out your years.

Cook Ting was cutting up an ox for Lord Wen-hui.[2] At every touch of his hand, every heave of his shoulder, every move of his feet, every thrust of his knee—zip! zoop! He slithered the knife along with a zing, and all was in perfect rhythm, as though he were performing the dance of the Mulberry Grove or keeping time to the Ching-shou music.[3]

"Ah, this is marvelous!" said Lord Wen-hui. "Imagine skill reaching such heights!"

Cook Ting laid down his knife and replied, "What I care about is the Way, which goes beyond skill. When I first began cutting up oxen, all I could see was the ox itself. After three years I no longer saw the whole ox. And now—now I go at it by spirit and don't look with my eyes. Perception and under-

[1] The chapter is very brief and would appear to be mutilated.
[2] Identified as King Hui of Wei, who has already appeared on p. 28 above.
[3] The Mulberry Grove is identified as a rain dance from the time of King T'ang of the Shang dynasty, and the Ching-shou music as part of a longer composition from the time of Yao.

standing have come to a stop and spirit moves where it wants. I go along with the natural makeup, strike in the big hollows, guide the knife through the big openings, and follow things as they are. So I never touch the smallest ligament or tendon, much less a main joint.

"A good cook changes his knife once a year—because he cuts. A mediocre cook changes his knife once a month—because he hacks. I've had this knife of mine for nineteen years and I've cut up thousands of oxen with it, and yet the blade is as good as though it had just come from the grindstone. There are spaces between the joints, and the blade of the knife has really no thickness. If you insert what has no thickness into such spaces, then there's plenty of room—more than enough for the blade to play about in. That's why after nineteen years the blade of my knife is still as good as when it first came from the grindstone.

"However, whenever I come to a complicated place, I size up the difficulties, tell myself to watch out and be careful, keep my eyes on what I'm doing, work very slowly, and move the knife with the greatest subtlety, until—flop! the whole thing comes apart like a clod of earth crumbling to the ground. I stand there holding the knife and look all around me, completely satisfied and reluctant to move on, and then I wipe off the knife and put it away." [4]

"Excellent!" said Lord Wen-hui. "I have heard the words of Cook Ting and learned how to care for life!"

[4] Waley (*Three Ways of Thought in Ancient China*, p. 73) takes this whole paragraph to refer to the working methods of a mediocre carver, and hence translates it very differently. There is a great deal to be said for his interpretation, but after much consideration I have decided to follow the traditional interpretation because it seems to me that the extreme care and caution which the cook uses *when he comes to a difficult place* is also a part of Chuang Tzu's "secret of caring for life."

When Kung-wen Hsüan saw the Commander of the Right,[5] he was startled and said, "What kind of man is this? How did he come to lose his foot? Was it Heaven? Or was it man?"

"It was Heaven, not man," said the commander. "When Heaven gave me life, it saw to it that I would be one-footed. Men's looks are given to them. So I know this was the work of Heaven and not of man. The swamp pheasant has to walk ten paces for one peck and a hundred paces for one drink, but it doesn't want to be kept in a cage. Though you treat it like a king, its spirit won't be content."

When Lao Tan[6] died, Ch'in Shih went to mourn for him; but after giving three cries, he left the room.

"Weren't you a friend of the Master?" asked Lao Tzu's disciples.

"Yes."

"And you think it's all right to mourn him this way?"

"Yes," said Ch'in Shih. "At first I took him for a real man, but now I know he wasn't. A little while ago, when I went in to mourn, I found old men weeping for him as though they were weeping for a son, and young men weeping for him as though they were weeping for a mother. To have gathered a group like *that*, he must have done something to make them talk about him, though he didn't ask them to talk, or make them weep for him, though he didn't ask them to weep. This is to hide from Heaven, turn your back on the true state of affairs, and forget what you were born with. In the old days, this was called the crime of hiding from Heaven. Your master

---

[5] Probably the ex-Commander of the Right, as he has been punished by having one foot amputated, a common penalty in ancient China. It is mutilating punishments such as these which Chuang Tzu has in mind when he talks about the need to "stay in one piece."

[6] Lao Tzu, the reputed author of the *Tao-te-ching*.

happened to come because it was his time, and he happened to leave because things follow along. If you are content with the time and willing to follow along, then grief and joy have no way to enter in. In the old days, this was called being freed from the bonds of God.

"Though the grease burns out of the torch, the fire passes on, and no one knows where it ends." [7]

[7] The first part of this last sentence is scarcely intelligible and there are numerous suggestions on how it should be interpreted or emended. I follow Chu Kuei-yao in reading "grease" instead of "finger." For the sake of reference, I list some of the other possible interpretations as I understand them. "When the fingers complete the work of adding firewood, the fire passes on" (Kuo Hsiang). "Though the fingers are worn out gathering firewood, the fire passes on" (Yü Yüeh). "What we can point to are the fagots that have been consumed; but the fire is transmitted elsewhere" (Legge, Fukunaga).

Yen Hui went to see Confucius and asked permission to take a trip.[1]

"Where are you going?"

"I'm going to Wei."

"What will you do there?"

"I have heard that the ruler of Wei is very young. He acts in an independent manner, thinks little of how he rules his state, and fails to see his faults. It is nothing to him to lead his people into peril, and his dead are reckoned by swampfuls like so much grass.[2] His people have nowhere to turn. I have heard you say, Master, 'Leave the state that is well ordered and go to the state in chaos! At the doctor's gate are many sick men.' I want to use these words as my standard, in hopes that I can restore his state to health."

"Ah," said Confucius, "you will probably go and get yourself executed, that's all. The Way doesn't want things mixed in with it. When it becomes a mixture, it becomes many ways; with many ways, there is a lot of bustle; and where there is a lot of bustle, there is trouble—trouble that has no remedy! The Perfect Man of ancient times made sure that he had it in him-

---

[1] Yen Hui was Confucius' favorite disciple. Throughout this chapter Chuang Tzu refers to a number of historical figures, many of whom appear in the *Analects*, though the speeches and anecdotes which he invents for them have nothing to do with history.

[2] Omitting the *kuo*, following Hsi T'ung. But there are many other interpretations of this peculiar sentence.

self before he tried to give it to others. When you're not even sure what you've got in yourself, how do you have time to bother about what some tyrant is doing?

"Do you know what it is that destroys virtue, and where wisdom comes from? Virtue is destroyed by fame, and wisdom comes out of wrangling. Fame is something to beat people down with, and wisdom is a device for wrangling. Both are evil weapons—not the sort of thing to bring you success. Though your virtue may be great and your good faith unassailable, if you do not understand men's spirits, though your fame may be wide and you do not strive with others, if you do not understand men's minds, but instead appear before a tyrant and force him to listen to sermons on benevolence and righteousness, measures and standards—this is simply using other men's bad points to parade your own excellence. You will be called a plaguer of others. He who plagues others will be plagued in turn. You will probably be plagued by this man.

"And suppose he is the kind who actually delights in worthy men and hates the unworthy—then why does he need you to try to make him any different? You had best keep your advice to yourself! Kings and dukes always lord it over others and fight to win the argument. You will find your eyes growing dazed, your color changing, your mouth working to invent excuses, your attitude becoming more and more humble, until in your mind you end by supporting him. This is to pile fire on fire, to add water to water, and is called 'increasing the excessive.' If you give in at the beginning, there is no place to stop. Since your fervent advice is almost certain not to be believed, you are bound to die if you come into the presence of a tyrant.

"In ancient times Chieh put Kuan Lung-feng to death and Chou put Prince Pi Kan to death. Both Kuan Lung-feng and

Prince Pi Kan were scrupulous in their conduct, bent down to comfort and aid the common people, and used their positions as ministers to oppose their superiors. Therefore their rulers, Chieh and Chou, utilized their scrupulous conduct as a means to trap them, for they were too fond of good fame. In ancient times Yao attacked Ts'ung-chih and Hsü-ao, and Yü attacked Yu-hu, and these states were left empty and unpeopled, their rulers cut down. It was because they employed their armies constantly and never ceased their search for gain. All were seekers of fame or gain—have you alone not heard of them? Even the sages cannot cope with men who are after fame or gain, much less a person like you!

"However, you must have some plan in mind. Come, tell me what it is."

Yen Hui said, "If I am grave and empty-hearted, diligent and of one mind, won't that do?"

"Goodness, how could *that* do? You may put on a fine outward show and seem very impressive, but you can't avoid having an uncertain look on your face, any more than an ordinary man can.[3] And then you try to gauge this man's feelings and seek to influence his mind. But with him, what is called 'the virtue that advances a little each day' would not succeed, much less a great display of virtue! He will stick fast to his position and never be converted. Though he may make outward signs of agreement, inwardly he will not give it a thought! How could such an approach succeed?"

"Well then, suppose I am inwardly direct, outwardly compliant, and do my work through the examples of antiquity?

[3] I follow Ma Hsü-lun in taking this sentence to refer to Yen Hui. The older interpretation of Kuo Hsiang takes it to mean: "He (the ruler of Wei) puts on a fine outward show and is very overbearing; his expression is never fixed, and ordinary men do not try to oppose him."

By being inwardly direct, I can be the companion of Heaven. Being a companion of Heaven, I know that the Son of Heaven and I are equally the sons of Heaven. Then why would I use my words to try to get men to praise me, or try to get them not to praise me? A man like this, people call The Child. This is what I mean by being a companion of Heaven.

"By being outwardly compliant, I can be a companion of men. Lifting up the tablet, kneeling, bowing, crouching down —this is the etiquette of a minister. Everybody does it, so why shouldn't I? If I do what other people do, they can hardly criticize me. This is what I mean by being a companion of men.

"By doing my work through the examples of antiquity, I can be the companion of ancient times. Though my words may in fact be lessons and reproaches, they belong to ancient times and not to me. In this way, though I may be blunt, I cannot be blamed. This is what I mean by being a companion of antiquity. If I go about it in this way, will it do?"

Confucius said, "Goodness, how could *that* do? You have too many policies and plans and you haven't seen what is needed. You will probably get off without incurring any blame, yes. But that will be as far as it goes. How do you think you can actually convert him? You are still making the mind [4] your teacher!"

Yen Hui said, "I have nothing more to offer. May I ask the proper way?"

"You must fast!" said Confucius. "I will tell you what that means. Do you think it is easy to do anything while you have a mind? If you do, Bright Heaven will not sanction you."

Yen Hui said, "My family is poor. I haven't drunk wine or

[4] Not the natural or "given" mind, but the mind which makes artificial distinctions.

eaten any strong foods for several months. So can I be considered as having fasted?"

"That is the fasting one does before a sacrifice, not the fasting of the mind."

"May I ask what the fasting of the mind is?"

Confucius said, "Make your will one! Don't listen with your ears, listen with your mind. No, don't listen with your mind, but listen with your spirit. Listening stops with the ears, the mind stops with recognition, but spirit is empty and waits on all things. The Way gathers in emptiness alone. Emptiness is the fasting of the mind."

Yen Hui said, "Before I heard this, I was certain that I was Hui. But now that I have heard it, there is no more Hui. Can this be called emptiness?"

"That's all there is to it," said Confucius. "Now I will tell you. You may go and play in his bird cage, but never be moved by fame. If he listens, then sing; if not, keep still. Have no gate, no opening,[5] but make oneness your house and live with what cannot be avoided. Then you will be close to success.

"It is easy to keep from walking; the hard thing is to walk without touching the ground. It is easy to cheat when you work for men, but hard to cheat when you work for Heaven. You have heard of flying with wings, but you have never heard of flying without wings. You have heard of the knowledge that knows, but you have never heard of the knowledge that does not know. Look into that closed room, the empty chamber where brightness is born! Fortune and blessing gather where there is stillness. But if you do not keep still—this is what is called sitting but racing around.[6] Let your ears and eyes com-

[5] Following Chang Ping-lin, I read *tou* instead of *tu*.
[6] The body sits but the mind continues to race.

municate with what is inside, and put mind and knowledge on the outside. Then even gods and spirits will come to dwell, not to speak of men! This is the changing of the ten thousand things, the bond of Yü and Shun, the constant practice of Fu Hsi and Chi Ch'ü.[7] How much more should it be a rule for lesser men!"

Tzu-kao, duke of She,[8] who was being sent on a mission to Ch'i, consulted Confucius. "The king is sending me on a very important mission. Ch'i will probably treat me with great honor but will be in no hurry to do anything more. Even a commoner cannot be forced to act, much less one of the feudal lords. I am very worried about it. You once said to me, 'In all affairs, whether large or small, there are few men who reach a happy conclusion except through the Way. If you do not succeed, you are bound to suffer from the judgment of men. If you do succeed, you are bound to suffer from the yin and yang.[9] To suffer no harm whether you succeed or not—only the man who has virtue can do that.' I am a man who eats plain food that is simply cooked, so that no one ever complains of the heat in my kitchens.[10] Yet this morning I received my orders from the king and by evening I am gulping ice water— do you suppose I have developed some kind of internal fever? I have not even gone to Ch'i to see what the situation is like and already I am suffering from the yin and yang. And if I do not succeed, I am bound to suffer from the judgment of

[7] Mythical sage rulers.

[8] A high minister of Ch'u and relative of the king.

[9] The excitement and worry of success will upset the balance of the yin and yang within the body and bring about sickness.

[10] The latter part of the sentence is barely intelligible and the translation tentative. Legge's interpretation is ingenious, though strained: "In my diet I take what is coarse, and do not seek delicacies,—a man whose cookery does not require him to be using cooling drinks."

men. I will have both worries. As a minister, I am not capable of carrying out this mission. But perhaps you have some advice you can give me . . ."

Confucius said, "In the world, there are two great decrees: one is fate and the other is duty.[11] That a son should love his parents is fate—you cannot erase this from his heart. That a subject should serve his ruler is duty—there is no place he can go and be without his ruler, no place he can escape to between heaven and earth. These are called the great decrees. Therefore, to serve your parents and be content to follow them anywhere—this is the perfection of filial piety. To serve your ruler and be content to do anything for him—this is the peak of loyalty. And to serve your own mind so that sadness or joy do not sway or move it; to understand what you can do nothing about and to be content with it as with fate—this is the perfection of virtue. As a subject and a son, you are bound to find things you cannot avoid. If you act in accordance with the state of affairs and forget about yourself, then what leisure will you have to love life and hate death? Act in this way and you will be all right.

"I want to tell you something else I have learned. In all human relations, if the two parties are living close to each other, they may form a bond through personal trust. But if they are far apart, they must use words to communicate their loyalty, and words must be transmitted by someone. To transmit words that are either pleasing to both parties or infuriating to both parties is one of the most difficult things in the world. Where both parties are pleased, there must be some exaggeration of the good points; and where both parties are angered, there must be some exaggeration of the bad points. Anything that smacks of exaggeration is irresponsible. Where there is

[11] *Yi*, elsewhere translated as "righteousness."

irresponsibility, no one will trust what is said, and when that happens, the man who is transmitting the words will be in danger. Therefore the aphorism says, 'Transmit the established facts; do not transmit words of exaggeration.' If you do that, you will probably come out all right.

"When men get together to pit their strength in games of skill, they start off in a light and friendly mood, but usually end up in a dark and angry one, and if they go on too long they start resorting to various underhanded tricks. When men meet at some ceremony to drink, they start off in an orderly manner, but usually end up in disorder, and if they go on too long they start indulging in various irregular amusements. It is the same with all things. What starts out being sincere usually ends up being deceitful. What was simple in the beginning acquires monstrous proportions in the end.

"Words are like wind and waves; actions are a matter of gain and loss. Wind and waves are easily moved; questions of gain and loss easily lead to danger. Hence anger arises from no other cause than clever words and one-sided speeches. When animals face death, they do not care what cries they make; their breath comes in gasps and a wild fierceness is born in their hearts. [Men, too,] if you press them too hard, are bound to answer you with ill-natured hearts, though they do not know why they do so. If they themselves do not understand why they behave like this, then who knows where it will end?

"Therefore the aphorism says, 'Do not deviate from your orders; do not press for completion.' To go beyond the limit is excess; to deviate from orders or press for completion is a dangerous thing. A good completion takes a long time; a bad completion cannot be changed later. Can you afford to be careless?

"Just go along with things and let your mind move freely.

Resign yourself to what cannot be avoided and nourish what is within you—this is best. What more do you have to do to fulfill your mission? Nothing is as good as following orders (obeying fate)—that's how difficult it is!" [12]

Yen Ho, who had been appointed tutor to the crown prince, son of Duke Ling of Wei, went to consult Chü Po-yü.[13] "Here is this man who by nature is lacking in virtue. If I let him go on with his unruliness I will endanger the state. If I try to impose some rule on him, I will endanger myself. He knows enough to recognize the faults of others, but he doesn't know his own faults. What can I do with a man like this?"

"A very good question," said Chü Po-yü. "Be careful, be on your guard, and make sure that you yourself are in the right! In your actions it is best to follow along with him, and in your mind it is best to harmonize with him. However, these two courses involve certain dangers. Though you follow along, you don't want to be pulled into his doings, and though you harmonize, you don't want to be drawn out too far. If in your actions you follow along to the extent of being pulled in with him, then you will be overthrown, destroyed, wiped out, and brought to your knees. If in your mind you harmonize to the extent of being drawn out, then you will be talked about, named, blamed, and condemned. If he wants to be a child, be

---

[12] The phrase *chih ming* can be interpreted either as "following orders" or as "obeying fate," and both meanings are almost certainly intended. Since for Chuang Tzu obeying fate is an extremely easy thing to do, the last part of the sentence is ironic. Throughout this passage Confucius, while appearing to give advice on how to carry out a diplomatic mission, is in fact enunciating Chuang Tzu's code for successful behavior in general.

[13] Yen Ho was a scholar of Lu, Chü Po-yü a minister of Wei. The crown prince is the notorious K'uai-k'uei, who was forced to flee from Wei because he plotted to kill his mother. He reentered the state and seized the throne from his son in 481 B.C.

a child with him. If he wants to follow erratic ways, follow erratic ways with him. If he wants to be reckless, be reckless with him. Understand him thoroughly, and lead him to the point where he is without fault.[14]

"Don't you know about the praying mantis that waved its arms angrily in front of an approaching carriage, unaware that they were incapable of stopping it? Such was the high opinion it had of its talents. Be careful, be on your guard! If you offend him by parading your store of talents, you will be in danger!

"Don't you know how the tiger trainer goes about it? He doesn't dare give the tiger any living thing to eat for fear it will learn the taste of fury by killing it. He doesn't dare give it any whole thing to eat for fear it will learn the taste of fury by tearing it apart. He gauges the state of the tiger's appetite and thoroughly understands its fierce disposition. Tigers are a different breed from men, and yet you can train them to be gentle with their keepers by following along with them. The men who get killed are the ones who go against them.

"The horse lover will use a fine box to catch the dung and a giant clam shell to catch the stale. But if a mosquito or a fly lights on the horse and he slaps it at the wrong time, then the horse will break the bit, hurt its head, and bang its chest. The horse lover tries to think of everything, but his affection leads him into error. Can you afford to be careless?"

Carpenter Shih went to Ch'i and, when he got to Crooked Shaft, he saw a serrate oak standing by the village shrine. It

[14] Waley (*Three Ways of Thought in Ancient China*, p. 109) translates, "And if you probe him, do so in a part where his skin is not sore," taking the verb *ta*, which I have translated as "understand thoroughly," to refer to acupuncture.

was broad enough to shelter several thousand oxen and meas-
ured a hundred spans around, towering above the hills. The
lowest branches were eighty feet from the ground, and a dozen
or so of them could have been made into boats. There were
so many sightseers that the place looked like a fair, but the
carpenter didn't even glance around and went on his way
without stopping. His apprentice stood staring for a long time
and then ran after Carpenter Shih and said, "Since I first took
up my ax and followed you, Master, I have never seen timber
as beautiful as this. But you don't even bother to look, and go
right on without stopping. Why is that?"

"Forget it—say no more!" said the carpenter. "It's a worthless
tree! Make boats out of it and they'd sink; make coffins and
they'd rot in no time; make vessels and they'd break at once.
Use it for doors and it would sweat sap like pine; use it for
posts and the worms would eat them up. It's not a timber
tree—there's nothing it can be used for. That's how it got to
be that old!"

After Carpenter Shih had returned home, the oak tree
appeared to him in a dream and said, "What are you comparing me with? Are you comparing me with those useful trees?
The cherry apple, the pear, the orange, the citron, the rest of
those fructiferous trees and shrubs—as soon as their fruit is
ripe, they are torn apart and subjected to abuse. Their big
limbs are broken off, their little limbs are yanked around. Their
utility makes life miserable for them, and so they don't get to
finish out the years Heaven gave them, but are cut off in mid-
journey. They bring it on themselves—the pulling and tearing
of the common mob. And it's the same way with all other
things.

"As for me, I've been trying a long time to be of no use, and
though I almost died, I've finally got it. This is of great
use to me. If I had been of some use, would I ever have grown

this large? Moreover you and I are both of us things. What's the point of this—things condemning things? You, a worthless man about to die—how do you know I'm a worthless tree?"

When Carpenter Shih woke up, he reported his dream. His apprentice said, "If it's so intent on being of no use, what's it doing there at the village shrine?" [15]

"Shhh! Say no more! It's only *resting* there. If we carp and criticize, it will merely conclude that we don't understand it. Even if it weren't at the shrine, do you suppose it would be cut down? It protects itself in a different way from ordinary people. If you try to judge it by conventional standards, you'll be way off!"

Tzu-ch'i of Nan-po was wandering around the Hill of Shang when he saw a huge tree there, different from all the rest. A thousand teams of horses could have taken shelter under it and its shade would have covered them all. Tzu-ch'i said, "What tree is this? It must certainly have some extraordinary usefulness!" But, looking up, he saw that the smaller limbs were gnarled and twisted, unfit for beams or rafters, and looking down, he saw that the trunk was pitted and rotten and could not be used for coffins. He licked one of the leaves and it blistered his mouth and made it sore. He sniffed the odor and it was enough to make a man drunk for three days. "It turns out to be a completely unusable tree," said Tzu-ch'i, "and so it has been able to grow this big. Aha!—it is this unusableness that the Holy Man makes use of!"

The region of Ching-shih in Sung is fine for growing catalpas, cypresses, and mulberries. But those that are more than

---

[15] The shrine, or altar of the soil, was always situated in a grove of beautiful trees. So the oak was serving a purpose by lending an air of sanctity to the spot.

one or two arm-lengths around are cut down for people who want monkey perches; those that are three or four spans around are cut down for the ridgepoles of tall roofs;[16] and those that are seven or eight spans are cut down for the families of nobles or rich merchants who want side boards for coffins. So they never get to live out the years Heaven gave them, but are cut down in mid-journey by axes. This is the danger of being usable. In the Chieh sacrifice,[17] oxen with white foreheads, pigs with turned-up snouts, and men with piles cannot be offered to the river. This is something all the shamans know, and hence they consider them inauspicious creatures. But the Holy Man for the same reason considers them highly auspicious.

There's Crippled Shu—chin stuck down in his navel, shoulders up above his head, pigtail pointing at the sky, his five organs on the top, his two thighs pressing his ribs. By sewing and washing, he gets enough to fill his mouth; by handling a winnow and sifting out the good grain, he makes enough to feed ten people. When the authorities call out the troops, he stands in the crowd waving good-by; when they get up a big work party, they pass him over because he's a chronic invalid. And when they are doling out grain to the ailing, he gets three big measures and ten bundles of firewood. With a crippled body, he's still able to look after himself and finish out the years Heaven gave him. How much better, then, if he had crippled virtue!

[16] Following Ma Hsü-lun, I read *mien* (roof) in place of *ming*.

[17] Probably a spring sacrifice for the "dispelling (*chieh*) of sins," though there are other interpretations. Sacrifices of animals, and sometimes human beings, were made to the Lord of the River, the god of the Yellow River.

When Confucius visited Ch'u, Chieh Yü, the madman of Ch'u, wandered by his gate crying, "Phoenix, phoenix, how has virtue failed! The future you cannot wait for; the past you cannot pursue. When the world has the Way, the sage succeeds; when the world is without the Way, the sage survives. In times like the present, we do well to escape penalty. Good fortune is light as a feather, but nobody knows how to pick it up. Misfortune is heavy as the earth, but nobody knows how to stay out of its way. Leave off, leave off—this teaching men virtue! Dangerous, dangerous—to mark off the ground and run! Fool, fool—don't spoil my walking! I walk a crooked way—don't step on my feet. The mountain trees do themselves harm; the grease in the torch burns itself up. The cinnamon can be eaten and so it gets cut down; the lacquer tree can be used and so it gets hacked apart. All men know the use of the useful, but nobody knows the use of the useless!" [18]

[18] Chuang Tzu bases this passage on the somewhat similar anecdote and song of the madman Chieh Yü in *Analects* XVIII, 5.

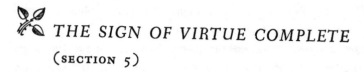

In Lu there was a man named Wang T'ai who had had his foot cut off.[1] He had as many followers gathered around him as Confucius.

Ch'ang Chi asked Confucius, "This Wang T'ai who's lost a foot—how does he get to divide up Lu with you, Master, and make half of it his disciples? He doesn't stand up and teach, he doesn't sit down and discuss, yet they go to him empty and come home full. Does he really have some wordless teaching, some formless way of bringing the mind to completion? What sort of man is he?"

Confucius said, "This gentleman is a sage. It's just that I've been tardy and haven't gone to see him yet. But if I go to him as my teacher, how much more should those who are not my equals! Why only the state of Lu? I'll bring the whole world along and we'll all become his followers!"

Ch'ang Chi said, "If he's lost a foot and is still superior to the Master, then how far above the common run of men he must be! But if that's so, then what unique way does he have of using his mind?"

Confucius said, "Life and death are great affairs, and yet they are no change to him. Though heaven and earth flop over and fall down, it is no loss to him. He sees clearly into what has no falsehood and does not shift with things. He takes it as

[1] As a penalty for some offense.

fate that things should change, and he holds fast to the source."

"What do you mean by that?" asked Ch'ang Chi.

Confucius said, "If you look at them from the point of view of their differences, then there is liver and gall, Ch'u and Yüeh. But if you look at them from the point of view of their sameness, then the ten thousand things are all one. A man like this doesn't know what his ears or eyes should approve—he lets his mind play in the harmony of virtue. As for things, he sees them as one and does not see their loss. He regards the loss of a foot as a lump of earth thrown away."

Ch'ang Chi said, "In the way he goes about it, he uses his knowledge to get at his mind, and uses his mind to get at the constant mind. Why should things gather around *him?*"

Confucius said, "Men do not mirror themselves in running water—they mirror themselves in still water. Only what is still can still the stillness of other things. Of those that receive life from the earth, the pine and cypress alone are best—they stay as green as ever in winter or summer. Of those that receive life from Heaven, Yao and Shun alone are best—they stand at the head of the ten thousand things. Luckily they were able to order their lives, and thereby order the lives of other things. Proof that a man is holding fast to the beginning lies in the fact of his fearlessness. A brave soldier will plunge alone into the midst of nine armies. He seeks fame and can bring himself to this. How much more, then, is possible for a man who governs Heaven and earth, stores up the ten thousand things, lets the six parts of his body[2] be only a dwelling, makes ornaments of his ears and eyes, unifies the knowledge of what he knows, and in his mind never tastes death. He will soon choose the day and ascend far off. Men may become his followers, but how could he be willing to bother himself about things?"

[2] The legs, arms, head, and trunk.

Shen-t'u Chia, who had lost a foot, was studying under Po-hun Wu-jen along with Tzu-ch'an of Cheng.[3] Tzu-ch'an said to Shen-t'u Chia, "If I go out first, you stay behind, and if you go out first, I'll stay behind."

Next day the two of them were again sitting on the same mat in the same hall. Tzu-ch'an said to Shen-t'u Chia, "If I go out first, you stay behind, and if you go out first, I'll stay behind! Now I will go out. Are you going to stay behind or aren't you? When you see a prime minister, you don't even get out of the way—do you think you're the equal of a prime minister?"

Shen-t'u Chia said, "Within the gates of the Master, is there any such thing as a prime minister? You take delight in being a prime minister and pushing people behind you. But I've heard that if the mirror is bright, no dust settles on it; if dust settles, it isn't really bright. When you live around worthy men a long time, you'll be free of faults. You regard the Master as a great man, and yet you talk like this—it's not right, is it?"

Tzu-ch'an said, "You, a man like this—and still you claim to be better than a Yao! Take a look at your virtue and see if it's not enough to give you cause to reflect!"

Shen-t'u Chia said, "People who excuse their faults and claim they didn't deserve to be punished—there are lots of them. But those who don't excuse their faults and who admit they didn't deserve to be spared—they are few. To know what you can't do anything about, and to be content with it as you would with fate—only a man of virtue can do that. If you play around in front of Archer Yi's target, you're right in the way of the arrows, and if you don't get hit, it's a matter of fate. There are lots of men with two feet who laugh at me for

[3] Tzu-ch'an (d 522 B.C.) was prime minister of the state of Cheng.

having only one. It makes me boil with rage, but I come here to the Master's place and I feel calmed down again and go home. I don't know whether he washes me clean with goodness, or whether I come to understand things by myself. The Master and I have been friends for nineteen years and he's never once let on that he's aware I'm missing a foot. Now you and I are supposed to be wandering outside the realm of forms and bodies, and you come looking for me inside it[4]—you're at fault, aren't you?"

Tzu-ch'an squirmed, changed his expression, and put a different look on his face. "Say no more about it," he said.

In Lu there was a man named Shu-shan No-Toes who had had his foot cut off. Stumping along, he went to see Confucius.

"You weren't careful enough!" said Confucius. "Since you've already broken the law and gotten yourself into trouble like this, what do you expect to gain by coming to me now?"

No-Toes said, "I just didn't understand my duty and was too careless of my body, and so I lost a foot. But I've come now because I still have something that is worth more than a foot and I want to try to hold on to it. There is nothing that heaven doesn't cover, nothing that earth doesn't bear up. I supposed, Master, that you would be like heaven and earth. How did I know you would act like this?"

"It was stupid of me," said Confucius. "Please, sir, won't you come in? I'd like to describe to you what I have learned."

But No-Toes went out.

Confucius said, "Be diligent, my disciples! Here is No-Toes, a man who has had his foot cut off, and still he's striving to

[4] Following the suggestion of Wang Mao-hung, I reverse the position of *nei* and *wai*.

learn so he can make up for the evil of his former conduct. How much more, then, should men whose virtue is still unimpaired!"

No-Toes told the story to Lao Tan. "Confucius certainly hasn't reached the stage of a Perfect Man, has he? What does he mean coming around so obsequiously to study with you? [5] He is after the sham illusion of fame and reputation and doesn't know that the Perfect Man looks on these as so many handcuffs and fetters!"

Lao Tan said, "Why don't you just make him see that life and death are the same story, that acceptable and unacceptable are on a single string? Wouldn't it be well to free him from his handcuffs and fetters?"

No-Toes said, "When Heaven has punished him, how can you set him free?"

Duke Ai of Lu said to Confucius, "In Wei there was an ugly man named Ai T'ai-t'o. But when men were around him, they thought only of him and couldn't break away, and when women saw him, they ran begging to their fathers and mothers, saying, 'I'd rather be this gentleman's concubine than another man's wife!'—there were more than ten such cases and it hasn't stopped yet. No one ever heard him take the lead—he always just chimed in with other people. He wasn't in the position of a ruler where he could save men's lives, and he had no store of provisions to fill men's bellies. On top of that, he was ugly enough to astound the whole world, chimed in but never led, and knew no more than what went on right around him. And yet men and women flocked to him. He certainly must be different from other men, I thought, and I

---

[5] The meaning is doubtful. I follow Kuo Hsiang in taking it to be a reference to the legend that Confucius went to Lao Tzu for instruction.

summoned him so I could have a look. Just as they said—he was ugly enough to astound the world. But he hadn't been with me more than a month or so when I began to realize what kind of man he was, and before the year was out, I really trusted him. There was no one in the state to act as chief minister, and I wanted to hand the government over to him. He was vague about giving an answer, evasive, as though he hoped to be let off, and I was embarrassed, but in the end I turned the state over to him. Then, before I knew it, he left me and went away. I felt completely crushed, as though I'd suffered a loss and didn't have anyone left to enjoy my state with. What kind of man is he anyway?"

Confucius said, "I once went on a mission to Ch'u, and as I was going along, I saw some little pigs nursing at the body of their dead mother. After a while, they gave a start and all ran away and left her, because they could no longer see their likeness in her, she was not the same. In loving their mother, they loved not her body but the thing that moved her body. When a man has been killed in battle and people come to bury him, he has no use for his medals. When a man has had his feet amputated, he doesn't care much about shoes. For both, the thing that is basic no longer exists. When women are selected to be consorts of the Son of Heaven, their nails are not pared and their ears are not pierced. When a man has just taken a wife, he is kept in posts outside [the palace] and is no longer sent on [dangerous] missions.[6] If so much care is taken to keep the body whole, how much more in the case of a man whose virtue is whole? Now Ai T'ai-t'o says nothing and is trusted, accomplishes nothing and is loved, so that people

---

[6] The sentence is unclear. Another interpretation would be: "he is allowed to spend nights at home and is not required to sleep in the officials' dormitory."

want to turn over their states to him and are only afraid he won't accept. It must be that his powers are whole, though his virtue takes no form."

"What do you mean when you say his powers are whole?" asked Duke Ai.

Confucius said, "Life, death, preservation, loss, failure, success, poverty, riches, worthiness, unworthiness, slander, fame, hunger, thirst, cold, heat—these are the alternations of the world, the workings of fate. Day and night they change place before us and wisdom cannot spy out their source. Therefore, they should not be enough to destroy your harmony; they should not be allowed to enter the storehouse of spirit. If you can harmonize and delight in them, master them and never be at a loss for joy, if you can do this day and night without break and make it be spring with everything, mingling with all and creating the moment within your own mind—this is what I call being whole in power."

"What do you mean when you say his virtue takes no form?"

"Among level things, water at rest is the most perfect, and therefore it can serve as a standard. It guards what is inside and shows no movement outside. Virtue is the establishment of perfect harmony. Though virtue takes no form, things cannot break away from it."

Some days later, Duke Ai reported his conversation to Min Tzu.[7] "At first, when I faced south and became ruler of the realm, I tried to look after the regulation of the people and worried that they might die. I really thought I understood things perfectly. But now that I've heard the words of a Perfect Man, I'm afraid there was nothing to my understanding—I was thinking too little of my own welfare and ruining

[7] A disciple of Confucius.

the state. Confucius and I are not subject and ruler—we are friends in virtue, that's all."

Mr. Lame-Hunchback-No-Lips talked to Duke Ling of Wei, and Duke Ling was so pleased with him that when he looked at normal men he thought their necks looked too lean and skinny.[8] Mr. Pitcher-Sized-Wen talked to Duke Huan of Ch'i, and Duke Huan was so pleased with him that when he looked at normal men he thought their necks looked too lean and skinny. Therefore, if virtue is preeminent, the body will be forgotten. But when men do not forget what can be forgotten, but forget what cannot be forgotten—that may be called true forgetting.

So the sage has his wanderings. For him, knowledge is an offshoot, promises are glue, favors are a patching up, and skill is a peddler. The sage hatches no schemes, so what use has he for knowledge? He does no carving, so what use has he for glue? He suffers no loss, so what use has he for favors? He hawks no goods, so what use has he for peddling? These four are called Heavenly Gruel. Heavenly Gruel is the food of Heaven, and if he's already gotten food from Heaven, what use does he have for men? He has the form of a man but not the feelings of a man. Since he has the form of a man, he bands together with other men. Since he doesn't have the feelings of a man, right and wrong cannot get at him. Puny and small, he sticks with the rest of men. Massive and great, he perfects his Heaven alone.

[8] Originally the text probably had some other phrase at this point referring to the walk, back, or lips of normal men, which dropped out and was replaced by the phrase from the parallel sentence that follows.

Hui Tzu said to Chuang Tzu, "Can a man really be without feelings?"

Chuang Tzu: "Yes."

Hui Tzu: "But a man who has no feelings—how can you call him a man?"

Chuang Tzu: "The Way gave him a face; Heaven gave him a form—why can't you call him a man?"

Hui Tzu: "But if you've already called him a man, how can he be without feelings?"

Chuang Tzu: "That's not what I mean by feelings. When I talk about having no feelings, I mean that a man doesn't allow likes or dislikes to get in and do him harm. He just lets things be the way they are and doesn't try to help life along."

Hui Tzu: "If he doesn't try to help life along, then how can he keep himself alive?"

Chuang Tzu: "The Way gave him a face; Heaven gave him a form. He doesn't let likes or dislikes get in and do him harm. You, now—you treat your spirit like an outside. You wear out your energy, leaning on a tree and moaning, slumping at your desk and dozing—Heaven picked out a body for you and you use it to gibber about 'hard' and 'white'!"[9]

---

* On "hard" and "white," see above, p. 37, n. 9. Chuang Tzu's description of Hui Tzu is rhymed in the original.

THE GREAT AND VENERABLE TEACHER

He who knows what it is that Heaven does, and knows what it is that man does, has reached the peak. Knowing what it is that Heaven does, he lives with Heaven. Knowing what it is that man does, he uses the knowledge of what he knows to help out the knowledge of what he doesn't know, and lives out the years that Heaven gave him without being cut off midway—this is the perfection of knowledge.

However, there is a difficulty. Knowledge must wait for something before it can be applicable, and that which it waits for is never certain. How, then, can I know that what I call Heaven is not really man, and what I call man is not really Heaven? There must first be a True Man[1] before there can be true knowledge.

What do I mean by a True Man? The True Man of ancient times did not rebel against want, did not grow proud in plenty, and did not plan his affairs. A man like this could commit an error and not regret it, could meet with success and not make a show. A man like this could climb the high places and not be frightened, could enter the water and not get wet, could enter the fire and not get burned. His knowledge was able to climb all the way up to the Way like this.

The True Man of ancient times slept without dreaming

[1] Another term for the Taoist sage, synonymous with the Perfect Man or the Holy Man.

and woke without care; he ate without savoring and his breath came from deep inside. The True Man breathes with his heels; the mass of men breathe with their throats. Crushed and bound down, they gasp out their words as though they were retching. Deep in their passions and desires, they are shallow in the workings of Heaven.

The True Man of ancient times knew nothing of loving life, knew nothing of hating death. He emerged without delight; he went back in without a fuss. He came briskly, he went briskly, and that was all. He didn't forget where he began; he didn't try to find out where he would end. He received something and took pleasure in it; he forgot about it and handed it back again. This is what I call not using the mind to repel the Way, not using man to help out Heaven. This is what I call the True Man.

Since he is like this, his mind forgets;[2] his face is calm; his forehead is broad. He is chilly like autumn, balmy like spring, and his joy and anger prevail through the four seasons. He goes along with what is right for things and no one knows his limit. Therefore, when the sage calls out the troops, he may overthrow nations but he will not lose the hearts of the people. His bounty enriches ten thousand ages but he has no love for men. Therefore he who delights in bringing success to things is not a sage; he who has affections is not benevolent; he who looks for the right time is not a worthy man; he who cannot encompass both profit and loss is not a gentleman; he who thinks of conduct and fame and misleads himself is not a man of breeding; and he who destroys himself and is without truth is not a user of men. Those like Hu Pu-hsieh, Wu Kuang, Po Yi, Shu Ch'i, Chi Tzu,

[2] Reading *wang* instead of *chih* in accordance with the suggestion of Wang Mao-hung.

Hsü Yü, Chi T'o, and Shen-t'u Ti—all of them slaved in the service of other men, took joy in bringing other men joy, but could not find joy in any joy of their own.[3]

This was the True Man of old: his bearing was lofty and did not crumble; he appeared to lack but accepted nothing; he was dignified in his correctness but not inisistent; he was vast in his emptiness but not ostentatious. Mild and cheerful, he seemed to be happy; reluctant, he could not help doing certain things; annoyed, he let it show in his face; relaxed, he rested in his virtue. Tolerant,[4] he seemed to be part of the world; towering alone, he could be checked by nothing; withdrawn, he seemed to prefer to cut himself off; bemused, he forgot what he was going to say.[5]

He regarded penalties as the body, rites as the wings, wisdom as what is timely, virtue as what is reasonable. Because he regarded penalties as the body, he was benign in his killing. Because he regarded rites as the wings, he got along in the world. Because he regarded wisdom as what is timely, there were things that he could not keep from doing. Because he regarded virtue as what is reasonable, he was like a man with two feet who gets to the top of the hill. And yet people really believed that he worked hard to get there.[6]

Therefore his liking was one and his not liking was one.

[3] According to legend, these were men who either tried to reform the conduct of others or made a show of guarding their own integrity. All either were killed or committed suicide.

[4] Following the Ts'ui text, which reads *kuang*.

[5] There are many different interpretations of the words used to describe the True Man in this paragraph. I have followed those adopted by Fukunaga.

[6] As pointed out by Fukunaga, this paragraph, which describes the Taoist sage as a ruler who employs penalties, rites, wisdom, and virtue, seems out of keeping with Chuang Tzu's philosophy as expressed elsewhere. Fukunaga suggests that it is an addition by a writer of the 3d or 2d centuries B.C. who was influenced by Legalist thought.

His being one was one and his not being one was one. In being one, he was acting as a companion of Heaven. In not being one, he was acting as a companion of man. When man and Heaven do not defeat each other, then we may be said to have the True Man.

Life and death are fated—constant as the succession of dark and dawn, a matter of Heaven. There are some things which man can do nothing about—all are a matter of the nature of creatures. If a man is willing to regard Heaven as a father and to love it, then how much more should he be willing to do for that which is even greater! [7] If he is willing to regard the ruler as superior to himself and to die for him, then how much more should he be willing to do for the Truth!

When the springs dry up and the fish are left stranded on the ground, they spew each other with moisture and wet each other down with spit—but it would be much better if they could forget each other in the rivers and lakes. Instead of praising Yao and condemning Chieh, it would be better to forget both of them and transform yourself with the Way.

The Great Clod burdens me with form, labors me with life, eases me in old age, and rests me in death. So if I think well of my life, for the same reason I must think well of my death. [8]

You hide your boat in the ravine and your fish net [9] in the swamp and tell yourself that they will be safe. But in the middle of the night a strong man shoulders them and carries

[7] Since Chuang Tzu elsewhere uses *T'ien* or Heaven as a synonym of the Way, this passage has troubled commentators. Some would emend the order of the words to read "If a man is willing to regard his father as Heaven," or would substitute *jen* for *T'ien*, that is, "If a man is willing to regard another man as his father."

[8] Or perhaps the meaning is: "So if it makes my life good, it must for the same reason make my death good."

[9] Following the interpretation of Yü Yüen.

them off, and in your stupidity you don't know why it happened. You think you do right to hide little things in big ones, and yet they get away from you. But if you were to hide the world in the world, so that nothing could get away, this would be the final reality of the constancy of things.

You have had the audacity to take on human form and you are delighted. But the human form has ten thousand changes that never come to an end. Your joys, then, must be uncountable. Therefore, the sage wanders in the realm where things cannot get away from him, and all are preserved. He delights in early death; he delights in old age; he delights in the beginning; he delights in the end. If he can serve as a model for men, how much more so that which the ten thousand things are tied to and all changes alike wait upon!

The Way has its reality and its signs but is without action or form. You can hand it down but you cannot receive it; you can get it but you cannot see it. It is its own source, its own root. Before Heaven and earth existed it was there, firm from ancient times. It gave spirituality to the spirits and to God; it gave birth to Heaven and to earth. It exists beyond the highest point, and yet you cannot call it lofty; it exists beneath the limit of the six directions, and yet you cannot call it deep. It was born before Heaven and earth, and yet you cannot say it has been there for long; it is earlier than the earliest time, and yet you cannot call it old.

Hsi-wei got it and held up heaven and earth.[10] Fu-hsi got it and entered into the mother of breath. The Big Dipper got it and from ancient times has never wavered. The Sun and Moon got it and from ancient times have never rested. K'an-

[10] The figures in this paragraph are all deities or mythical beings, but the myths to which Chuang Tzu refers are in many cases unknown, so that the translation is tentative in places.

p'i got it and entered K'un-lun. P'ing-i got it and wandered in the great river. Chien Wu got it and lived in the great mountain.[11] The Yellow Emperor got it and ascended to the cloudy heavens. Chuan Hsü got it and dwelt in the Dark Palace. Yü-ch'iang got it and stood at the limit of the north. The Queen Mother of the West got it and took her seat on Shao-kuang—nobody knows her beginning, nobody knows her end. P'eng-tsu got it and lived from the age of Shun to the age of the Five Dictators.[12] Fu Yüeh got it and became minister to Wu-ting, who extended his rule over the whole world; then Fu Yüeh climbed up to the Eastern Governor, straddled the Winnowing Basket and the Tail, and took his place among the ranks of stars.[13]

Nan-po Tzu-k'uei said to the Woman Crookback, "You are old in years and yet your complexion is that of a child. Why is this?"

"I have heard the Way!"

"Can the Way be learned?" asked Nan-po Tzu-k'uei.

"Goodness, how could that be? Anyway, you aren't the man to do it. Now there's Pu-liang Yi—he has the talent of a sage but not the Way of a sage, whereas I have the Way of a sage but not the talent of a sage. I thought I would try to teach him and see if I could really get anywhere near to making him a

[11] K'an-p'i is the god of the mythical K'un-lun Mountains of the west, P'ing-i is the god of the Yellow River, and Chien Wu is the god of Mount T'ai.

[12] The Yellow Emperor and Chuan Hsü are legendary rulers. The Queen Mother of the West is an immortal spirit who lives in the far west. Yü-ch'iang is a deity of the far north. P'eng-tsu's life span as given here extends, by traditional dating, from the 26th to the 7th centuries B.C.

[13] Fu Yüeh is frequently mentioned as a minister to the Shang ruler Wu-ting (traditional dates 1324–1266 B.C.), but little is known of the legend that he ascended to the sky and became a star.

sage. It's easier to explain the Way of a sage to someone who has the talent of a sage, you know. So I began explaining and kept at him for three days,[14] and after that he was able to put the world outside himself. When he had put the world outside himself, I kept at him for seven days more, and after that he was able to put things outside himself. When he had put things outside himself, I kept at him for nine days more, and after that he was able to put life outside himself. After he had put life outside himself, he was able to achieve the brightness of dawn, and when he had achieved the brightness of dawn, he could see his own aloneness. After he had managed to see his own aloneness, he could do away with past and present, and after he had done away with past and present, he was able to enter where there is no life and no death. That which kills life does not die; that which gives life to life does not live.[15] This is the kind of thing it is: there's nothing it doesn't send off, nothing it doesn't welcome, nothing it doesn't destroy, nothing it doesn't complete. Its name is Peace-in-Strife. After the strife, it attains completion."

Nan-po Tzu-k'uei asked, "Where did you happen to hear this?"

"I heard it from the son of Aided-by-Ink, and Aided-by-Ink heard it from the grandson of Repeated-Recitation, and the grandson of Repeated-Recitation heard it from Seeing-Brightly, and Seeing-Brightly heard it from Whispered-Agreement, and Whispered-Agreement heard it from Waiting-for-Use, and Waiting-for-Use heard it from Exclaimed-Wonder, and Exclaimed-Wonder heard it from Dark-Ob-

---

[14] Following the suggestion of Wen I-to, I reverse the position of *shou* and *kao*.

[15] I.e., that which transcends the categories of life and death can never be said to have lived or died; only that which recognizes the existence of such categories is subject to them.

scurity, and Dark-Obscurity heard it from Participation-in-Mystery, and Participation-in-Mystery heard it from Copy-the-Source!" [16]

Master Ssu, Master Yü, Master Li, and Master Lai were all four talking together. "Who can look upon nonbeing as his head, on life as his back, and on death as his rump?" they said. "Who knows that life and death, existence and annihilation, are all a single body? I will be his friend!"

The four men looked at each other and smiled. There was no disagreement in their hearts and so the four of them became friends.

All at once Master Yü fell ill. Master Ssu went to ask how he was. "Amazing!" said Master Yü. "The Creator is making me all crookedy like this! My back sticks up like a hunchback and my vital organs are on top of me. My chin is hidden in my navel, my shoulders are up above my head, and my pigtail points at the sky. It must be some dislocation of the yin and yang!"

Yet he seemed calm at heart and unconcerned. Dragging himself haltingly to the well, he looked at his reflection and said, "My, my! So the Creator is making me all crookedy like this!"

"Do you resent it?" asked Master Ssu.

"Why no, what would I resent? If the process continues, perhaps in time he'll transform my left arm into a rooster. In that case I'll keep watch on the night. Or perhaps in time he'll transform my right arm into a crossbow pellet and I'll

---

[16] Reading *ni-shih* instead of *i-shih* for the last name. But these names are open to a variety of interpretations. The whole list, of course, is a parody of the filiations of the other schools of philosophy.

shoot down an owl for roasting. Or perhaps in time he'll transform my buttocks into cartwheels. Then, with my spirit for a horse, I'll climb up and go for a ride. What need will I ever have for a carriage again?

"I received life because the time had come; I will lose it because the order of things passes on. Be content with this time and dwell in this order and then neither sorrow nor joy can touch you. In ancient times this was called the 'freeing of the bound.' There are those who cannot free themselves, because they are bound by things. But nothing can ever win against Heaven—that's the way it's always been. What would I have to resent?"

Suddenly Master Lai grew ill. Gasping and wheezing, he lay at the point of death. His wife and children gathered round in a circle and began to cry. Master Li, who had come to ask how he was, said, "Shoo! Get back! Don't disturb the process of change!"

Then he leaned against the doorway and talked to Master Lai. "How marvelous the Creator is! What is he going to make out of you next? Where is he going to send you? Will he make you into a rat's liver? Will he make you into a bug's arm?"

Master Lai said, "A child, obeying his father and mother, goes wherever he is told, east or west, south or north. And the yin and yang—how much more are they to a man than father or mother! Now that they have brought me to the verge of death, if I should refuse to obey them, how perverse I would be! What fault is it of theirs? The Great Clod burdens me with form, labors me with life, eases me in old age, and rests me in death. So if I think well of my life, for the same reason I must think well of my death. When a skilled smith is casting metal, if the metal should leap up and say,

'I insist upon being made into a Mo-yeh!' [17] he would surely regard it as very inauspicious metal indeed. Now, having had the audacity to take on human form once, if I should say, 'I don't want to be anything but a man! Nothing but a man!', the Creator would surely regard me as a most inauspicious sort of person. So now I think of heaven and earth as a great furnace, and the Creator as a skilled smith. Where could he send me that would not be all right? I will go off to sleep peacefully, and then with a start I will wake up."

Master Sang-hu, Meng-tzu Fan, and Master Ch'in-chang, three friends, said to each other, "Who can join with others without joining with others? Who can do with others without doing with others? Who can climb up to heaven and wander in the mists, roam the infinite, and forget life forever and forever?" The three men looked at each other and smiled. There was no disagreement in their hearts and so they became friends.

After some time had passed without event, Master Sang-hu died. He had not yet been buried when Confucius, hearing of his death, sent Tzu-kung to assist at the funeral. When Tzu-kung arrived, he found one of the dead man's friends weaving frames for silkworms, while the other strummed a lute. Joining their voices, they sang this song:

> Ah, Sang-hu!
> Ah, Sang-hu!
> You have gone back to your true form
> While we remain as men, O!

Tzu-kung hastened forward and said, "May I be so bold as to ask what sort of ceremony this is—singing in the very presence of the corpse?"

The two men looked at each other and laughed. "What

[17] A famous sword of King Ho-lü (r. 514–496 B.C.) of Wu.

does this man know of the meaning of ceremony?" they said.

Tzu-kung returned and reported to Confucius what had happened. "What sort of men are they anyway?" he asked. "They pay no attention to proper behavior, disregard their personal appearance and, without so much as changing the expression on their faces, sing in the very presence of the corpse! I can think of no name for them! What sort of men are they?"

"Such men as they," said Confucius, "wander beyond the realm; men like me wander within it. Beyond and within can never meet. It was stupid of me to send you to offer condolences. Even now they have joined with the Creator as men to wander in the single breath of heaven and earth. They look upon life as a swelling tumor, a protruding wen, and upon death as the draining of a sore or the bursting of a boil. To men such as these, how could there be any question of putting life first or death last? They borrow the forms of different creatures and house them in the same body. They forget liver and gall, cast aside ears and eyes, turning and revolving, ending and beginning again, unaware of where they start or finish. Idly they roam beyond the dust and dirt; they wander free and easy in the service of inaction. Why should they fret and fuss about the ceremonies of the vulgar world and make a display for the ears and eyes of the common herd?"

Tzu-kung said, "Well then, Master, what is this 'realm' that you stick to?"

Confucius said, "I am one of those men punished by Heaven. Nevertheless, I will share with you what I have."

"Then may I ask about the realm?" [18] said Tzu-kung.

[18] The word *fang*, which I have translated as "realm," may also mean "method" or "procedure," and Confucius' answer seems to stress this latter meaning.

Confucius said, "Fish thrive in water, man thrives in the Way. For those that thrive in water, dig a pond and they will find nourishment enough. For those that thrive in the Way, don't bother about them and their lives will be secure. So it is said, the fish forget each other in the rivers and lakes, and men forget each other in the arts of the Way."

Tzu-kung said, "May I ask about the singular man?"

"The singular man is singular in comparison to other men, but a companion of Heaven. So it is said, the petty man of Heaven is a gentleman among men; the gentleman among men is the petty man of Heaven."

Yen Hui said to Confucius, "When Meng-sun Ts'ai's mother died, he wailed without shedding any tears, he did not grieve in his heart, and he conducted the funeral without any look of sorrow. He fell down on these three counts, and yet he is known all over the state of Lu for the excellent way he managed the funeral. Is it really possible to gain such a reputation when there are no facts to support it? I find it very peculiar indeed!"

Confucius said, "Meng-sun did all there was to do. He was advanced beyond ordinary understanding and he would have simplified things even more, but that wasn't practical. However, there is still a lot that he simplified. Meng-sun doesn't know why he lives and doesn't know why he dies. He doesn't know why he should go ahead; he doesn't know why he should fall behind. In the process of change, he has become a thing [among other things], and he is merely waiting for some other change that he doesn't yet know about. Moreover, when he is changing, how does he know that he is really changing? And when he is not changing, how does he know that he hasn't already changed? You and I, now—we are dreaming and haven't waked up yet. But in his case, though something may startle his body, it won't injure his mind; though something may alarm the house [his spirit lives in], his emotions will suffer no death. Meng-sun alone has waked up. Men wail and so he wails, too—that's the reason he acts like this.

"What's more, we go around telling each other, I do this, I do that—but how do we know that this 'I' we talk about has any 'I' to it? You dream you're a bird and soar up into the sky; you dream you're a fish and dive down in the pool. But now when you tell me about it, I don't know whether you are awake or whether you are dreaming. Running around accusing others[19] is not as good as laughing, and enjoying a good laugh is not as good as going along with things. Be content to go along and forget about change and then you can enter the mysterious oneness of Heaven."

Yi Erh-tzu went to see Hsü Yu.[20] Hsü Yu said, "What kind of assistance has Yao been giving you?"

Yi Erh-tzu said, "Yao told me, 'You must learn to practice benevolence and righteousness and to speak clearly about right and wrong!'"

"Then why come to see *me?*" said Hsü Yu. "Yao has already tattooed you with benevolence and righteousness and cut off your nose with right and wrong.[21] Now how do you

[19] Following Hsi T'ung, I read *tse* instead of *shih,* but the sentence is obscure and there are many interpretations.

[20] A recluse of the time of Emperor Yao. He has already appeared on p. 26 above.

[21] Tattooing and cutting off the nose were common punishments.

expect to go wandering in any far-away, carefree, and as-you-like-it paths?"

"That may be," said Yi Erh-tzu. "But I would like if I may to wander in a little corner of them."

"Impossible!" said Hsü Yu. "Eyes that are blind have no way to tell the loveliness of faces and features; eyes with no pupils have no way to tell the beauty of colored and embroidered silks."

Yi Erh-tzu said, "Yes, but Wu-chuang forgot her beauty, Chü-liang forgot his strength, and the Yellow Emperor forgot his wisdom—all were content to be recast and remolded.[22] How do you know that the Creator will not wipe away my tattoo, stick my nose back on again, and let me ride on the process of completion and follow after you, Master?"

"Ah—we can never tell," said Hsü Yu. "I will just speak to you about the general outline. This Teacher of mine, this Teacher of mine—he passes judgment on the ten thousand things but he doesn't think himself righteous; his bounty extends to ten thousand generations but he doesn't think himself benevolent. He is older than the highest antiquity but he doesn't think himself long-lived; he covers heaven, bears up the earth, carves and fashions countless forms, but he doesn't think himself skilled. It is with him alone I wander."

Yen Hui said, "I'm improving!"

Confucius said, "What do you mean by that?"

[22] Judging from the context, Wu-chuang and Chü-liang must have been noted for their beauty and strength respectively. Perhaps the former is the same as the beautiful Mao-ch'iang already mentioned on p. 41, above. All these persons forgot themselves in the Way and were remolded by the Creator.

"I've forgotten benevolence and righteousness!"

"That's good. But you still haven't got it."

Another day, the two met again and Yen Hui said, "I'm improving!"

"What do you mean by that?"

"I've forgotten rites and music!"

"That's good. But you still haven't got it."

Another day, the two met again and Yen Hui said, "I'm improving!"

"What do you mean by that?"

"I can sit down and forget everything!"

Confucius looked very startled and said, "What do you mean, sit down and forget everything?"

Yen Hui said, "I smash up my limbs and body, drive out perception and intellect, cast off form, do away with understanding, and make myself identical with the Great Thoroughfare. This is what I mean by sitting down and forgetting everything."

Confucius said, "If you're identical with it, you must have no more likes! If you've been transformed, you must have no more constancy! So you really are a worthy man after all! [23] With your permission, I'd like to become your follower."

Master Yü and Master Sang were friends. Once it rained incessantly for ten days. Master Yü said to himself, Master Sang is probably having a bad time, and he wrapped up some rice and took it for his friend to eat. When he got to Master

---

[23] Chuang Tzu probably intends a humorous reference to the words of Confucius in *Analects* VI, 9: "The Master said, 'What a worthy man was Hui!'"

Sang's gate, he heard something like singing or crying, and someone striking a lute and saying:

> Father?
> Mother?
> Heaven?
> Man?

It was as though the voice would not hold out and the singer were rushing to get through the words.

Master Yü went inside and said, "What do you mean—singing a song like that!"

"I was pondering what it is that has brought me to this extremity, but I couldn't find the answer. My father and mother surely wouldn't wish this poverty on me. Heaven covers all without partiality; earth bears up all without partiality—heaven and earth surely wouldn't single me out to make me poor. I try to discover who is doing it, but I can't get the answer. Still, here I am—at the very extreme. It must be fate."

FIT FOR EMPERORS
AND KINGS
(SECTION 7)

Nieh Ch'üeh was questioning Wang Ni. Four times he asked a question and four times Wang Ni said he didn't know. Nieh Ch'üeh proceeded to hop around in great glee and went and told Master P'u-i. Master P'u-i said, "Are you just now finding *that* out?[1] The clansman Yu-yü was no match for the clansman T'ai.[2] The clansman Yu-yü still held on to benevolence and worked to win men over. He won men over all right, but he never got out into [the realm of] 'not-man.' The clansman T'ai, now—he lay down peaceful and easy; he woke up wide-eyed and blank. Sometimes he thought he was a horse; sometimes he thought he was a cow. His understanding was truly trustworthy; his virtue was perfectly true. He never entered [the realm of] 'not-man.' "[3]

Chien Wu went to see the madman Chieh Yü. Chieh Yü

[1] On Nieh Ch'üeh and Wang Ni, see above, pp. 40–42. Master P'u-i is probably the same as Master P'i-i, who appears elsewhere in the *Chuang Tzu* as the teacher of Wang Ni. According to commentators, Nieh Ch'üeh's delight came from the fact that he had finally realized that there are no answers to questions.

[2] "The clansman Yu-yü" is the sage ruler Shun, the ideal of the Confucian philosophers. "The clansman T'ai" is vaguely identified as a ruler of high antiquity.

[3] The existence of a category "not-man" depends upon the recognition of a category "man." Shun could get no further than the category "man"; hence he never reached the realm of "not-man." T'ai, on the other hand, was able to transcend all such categories.

said, "What was Chung Shih telling you the other day?" [4]

Chien Wu said, "He told me that the ruler of men should devise his own principles, standards, ceremonies, and regulations, and then there will be no one who will fail to obey him and be transformed by them."

The madman Chieh Yü said, "This is bogus virtue! To try to govern the world like this is like trying to walk the ocean, to drill through a river, or to make a mosquito shoulder a mountain! When the sage governs, does he govern what is on the *outside*? He makes sure of himself first, and then he acts. He makes absolutely certain that things can do what they are supposed to do, that is all. The bird flies high in the sky where it can escape the danger of stringed arrows. The field mouse burrows deep down under the sacred hill where it won't have to worry about men digging and smoking it out. Have you got less sense than these two little creatures?"

T'ien Ken was wandering on the sunny side of Yin Mountain. When he reached the banks of the Liao River, he happened to meet a Nameless Man. He questioned the man, saying, "Please may I ask how to rule the world?"

The Nameless Man said, "Get away from me, you peasant! What kind of a dreary question is that! I'm just about to set off with the Creator. And if I get bored with that, then I'll ride on the Light-and-Lissome Bird out beyond the six directions, wandering in the village of Not-Even-Anything and living in the Broad-and-Borderless field. What business[5] do

[4] Chien Wu and Chieh Yü have already appeared above, on p. 27. Nothing is known of Chung Shih. I follow Yü Yüeh in taking *jih* to mean "the other day."

you have coming with this talk of governing the world and disturbing my mind?"

But T'ien Ken repeated his question. The Nameless Man said, "Let your mind wander in simplicity, blend your spirit with the vastness, follow along with things the way they are, and make no room for personal views—then the world will be governed."

Yang-tzu Chü[6] went to see Lao Tan and said, "Here is a man swift as an echo, strong as a beam, with a wonderfully clear understanding of the principles of things, studying the Way without ever letting up—a man like this could compare with an enlightened king, couldn't he?"

Lao Tan said, "In comparison to the sage, a man like this is a drudging slave, a craftsman bound to his calling, wearing out his body, grieving his mind. They say it is the beautiful markings of the tiger and the leopard that call out the hunters, the nimbleness of the monkey and the ability of the dog to catch rats[7] that make them end up chained. A man like this —how could he compare to an enlightened king?"

Yang-tzu Chü, much taken aback, said, "May I venture to ask about the government of the enlightened king?"

Lao Tan said, "The government of the enlightened king? His achievements blanket the world but appear not to be his own doing. His transforming influence touches the ten thou-

---

[6] I follow the traditional interpretation, though in fact no one has succeeded in determining the meaning of this character for certain. Other interpretations are: "How do you have the leisure to come," etc., or "What is this dream talk that you come with about governing the world," etc.

[6] Perhaps meant to be identified with the hedonist philosopher Yang Chu.

[7] Reading *liu* in accordance with the parallel passage in Section 12.

sand things but the people do not depend on him. With him there is no promotion or praise—he lets everything find its own enjoyment. He takes his stand on what cannot be fathomed and wanders where there is nothing at all."

In Cheng there was a shaman of the gods named Chi Hsien. He could tell whether men would live or die, survive or perish, be fortunate or unfortunate, live a long time or die young, and he would predict the year, month, week,[8] and day as though he were a god himself. When the people of Cheng saw him, they dropped everything and ran out of his way. Lieh Tzu went to see him and was completely intoxicated. Returning, he said to Hu Tzu,[9] "I used to think, Master, that your Way was perfect. But now I see there is something even higher!"

Hu Tzu said, "I have already showed you all the outward forms, but I haven't yet showed you the substance—and do you really think you have mastered this Way of mine? There may be a flock of hens but, if there is no rooster, how can they lay fertile eggs? You take what you know of the Way and wave it in the face of the world, expecting to be believed! This is the reason men can see right through you. Try bringing your shaman along next time and letting him get a look at me."

The next day Lieh Tzu brought the shaman to see Hu Tzu. When they had left the room, the shaman said, "I'm so sorry—your master is dying! There's no life left in him—he won't last the week. I saw something very strange—something like wet ashes!"

Lieh Tzu went back into the room, weeping and drenching

[8] The ancient ten-day week.
[9] The Taoist philosopher Lieh Tzu has already appeared on p. 26 above. Hu Tzu is his teacher.

the collar of his robe with tears, and reported this to Hu Tzu.

Hu Tzu said, "Just now I appeared to him with the Pattern of Earth—still and silent, nothing moving, nothing standing up. He probably saw in me the Workings of Virtue Closed Off.[10] Try bringing him around again."

The next day the two came to see Hu Tzu again, and when they had left the room, the shaman said to Lieh Tzu, "It certainly was lucky that your master met me! He's going to get better—he has all the signs of life! I could see the stirring of what had been closed off!"

Lieh Tzu went in and reported this to Hu Tzu.

Hu Tzu said, "Just now I appeared to him as Heaven and Earth—no name or substance to it, but still the workings, coming up from the heels. He probably saw in me the Workings of the Good One.[11] Try bringing him again."

The next day the two came to see Hu Tzu again, and when they had left the room, the shaman said to Lieh Tzu, "Your master is never the *same!* I have no way to physiognomize him! If he will try to steady himself, then I will come and examine him again."

Lieh Tzu went in and reported this to Hu Tzu.

Hu Tzu said, "Just now I appeared to him as the Great Vastness Where Nothing Wins Out. He probably saw in me the Workings of the Balanced Breaths. Where the swirling waves[12] gather there is an abyss; where the still waters gather there is an abyss; where the running waters gather there is an

[10] Virtue here has the sense of vital force. Cf. *Book of Changes, Hsi tz'u* 2: "The Great Virtue of Heaven and Earth is called life."

[11] The language of this whole passage is, needless to say, deliberately mysterious. The term "Good One" may have some relation to the passage in the *Changes, Hsi tz'u* 1: "The succession of the yin and yang is called the Way. What carries it on is goodness."

[12] Following the emendation and interpretation of Ma Hsü-lun.

abyss. The abyss has nine names and I have shown him three.[13] Try bringing him again."

The next day the two came to see Hu Tzu again, but before the shaman had even come to a halt before Hu Tzu, his wits left him and he fled.

"Run after him!" said Hu Tzu, but though Lieh Tzu ran after him, he could not catch up. Returning, he reported to Hu Tzu, "He's vanished! He's disappeared! I couldn't catch up with him."

Hu Tzu said, "Just now I appeared to him as Not Yet Emerged from My Source. I came at him empty, wriggling and turning, not knowing anything about 'who' or 'what,' now dipping and bending, now flowing in waves—that's why he ran away."

After this, Lieh Tzu concluded that he had never really begun to learn anything.[14] He went home and for three years did not go out. He replaced his wife at the stove, fed the pigs as though he were feeding people, and showed no preferences in the things he did. He got rid of the carving and polishing and returned to plainness, letting his body stand alone like a clod. In the midst of entanglement he remained sealed, and in this oneness he ended his life.

Do not be an embodier of fame; do not be a storehouse of schemes; do not be an undertaker of projects; do not be a proprietor of wisdom. Embody to the fullest what has no end and wander where there is no trail. Hold on to all that you have received from Heaven but do not think you have gotten

[13] A   ling to commentators, the three forms of the abyss in the order given h e correspond to the third, first, and second of Hu Tzu's manifestations.

[14] That is, he had reached the highest stage of understanding.

anything. Be empty, that is all. The Perfect Man uses his mind like a mirror—going after nothing, welcoming nothing, responding but not storing. Therefore he can win out over things and not hurt himself.

The emperor of the South Sea was called Shu [Brief], the emperor of the North Sea was called Hu [Sudden], and the emperor of the central region was called Hun-tun [Chaos]. Shu and Hu from time to time came together for a meeting in the territory of Hun-tun, and Hun-tun treated them very generously. Shu and Hu discussed how they could repay his kindness. "All men," they said, "have seven openings so they can see, hear, eat, and breathe. But Hun-tun alone doesn't have any. Let's trying boring him some!"

Every day they bored another hole, and on the seventh day Hun-tun died.

 *AUTUMN FLOODS*

(SECTION 17)

The time of the autumn floods came and the hundred streams
poured into the Yellow River. Its racing current swelled to
such proportions that, looking from bank to bank or island to
island, it was impossible to distinguish a horse from a cow.
Then the Lord of the River[1] was beside himself with joy, be-
lieving that all the beauty in the world belonged to him alone.
Following the current, he journeyed east until at last he
reached the North Sea. Looking east, he could see no end to
the water.

The Lord of the River began to wag his head and roll his
eyes. Peering far off in the direction of Jo,[2] he sighed and said,
"The common saying has it, 'He has heard the Way a mere
hundred times but he thinks he's better than anyone else.' It
applies to me. In the past, I heard men belittling the learning
of Confucius and making light of the righteousness of Po Yi,[3]
though I never believed them. Now, however, I have seen
your unfathomable vastness. If I hadn't come to your gate,[4]
I should have been in danger. I should forever have been
laughed at by the masters of the Great Method!"

[1] The Lord of the River, the god of the Yellow River, has already appeared on p. 78, under the name P'ing-i.
[2] The god of the sea.
[3] Po Yi, who relinquished his kingdom to his brother and later chose to
die of starvation rather than serve a ruler he considered unjust, was regarded
as a model of righteousness.
[4] The Lord of the River has literally come to the gate of the sea. But a
second meaning is implied, that is, "If I hadn't become your disciple."

Jo of the North Sea said, "You can't discuss the ocean with a well frog—he's limited by the space he lives in. You can't discuss ice with a summer insect—he's bound to a single season. You can't discuss the Way with a cramped scholar—he's shackled by his doctrines. Now you have come out beyond your banks and borders and have seen the great sea—so you realize your own pettiness. From now on it will be possible to talk to you about the Great Principle.

"Of all the waters of the world, none is as great as the sea. Ten thousand streams flow into it—I have never heard of a time when they stopped—and yet it is never full. The water leaks away at Wei-lü[5]—I have never heard of a time when it didn't—and yet the sea is never empty. Spring or autumn, it never changes. Flood or drought, it takes no notice. It is so much greater than the streams of the Yangtze or the Yellow River that it is impossible to measure the difference. But I have never for this reason prided myself on it. I take my place with heaven and earth and receive breath from the yin and yang. I sit here between heaven and earth as a little stone or a little tree sits on a huge mountain. Since I can see my own smallness, what reason would I have to pride myself?

"Compare the area within the four seas with all that is between heaven and earth—is it not like one little anthill in a vast marsh? Compare the Middle Kingdom with the area within the four seas—is it not like one tiny grain in a great storehouse? When we refer to the things of creation, we speak of them as numbering ten thousand—and man is only one of them. We talk of the Nine Provinces where men are most numerous, and yet of the whole area where grain and foods are grown and where boats and carts pass back and forth, man oc-

[5] Said by some commentators to be a huge fiery stone against which the sea water turns to steam.

cupies only one fraction.[6] Compared to the ten thousand things, is he not like one little hair on the body of a horse? What the Five Emperors passed along, what the Three Kings fought over, what the benevolent man grieves about, what the responsible man labors over—all is no more than this! [7] Po Yi gained a reputation by giving it up; Confucius passed himself off as learned because he talked about it. But in priding themselves in this way, were they not like you a moment ago priding yourself on your flood waters?"

"Well then," said the Lord of the River, "if I recognize the hugeness of heaven and earth and the smallness of the tip of a hair, will that do?"

"No indeed!" said Jo of the North Sea. "There is no end to the weighing of things, no stop to time, no constancy to the division of lots, no fixed rule to beginning and end. Therefore great wisdom observes both far and near, and for that reason recognizes small without considering it paltry, recognizes large without considering it unwieldy, for it knows that there is no end to the weighing of things. It has a clear understanding of past and present, and for that reason it spends a long time without finding it tedious, a short time without fretting at its shortness, for it knows that time has no stop. It perceives the nature of fullness and emptiness, and for that reason it does not delight if it acquires something nor worry if it loses it, for it knows that there is no constancy to the division of lots. It comprehends the Level Road, and for that reason it does not

---

[6] As it stands in the original, this sentence makes little sense to me, and the translation represents no more than a tentative attempt to extract some meaning.

[7] The Five Emperors were five legendary rulers of high antiquity, of whom the Yellow Emperor, Yao, and Shun are the most famous. The Three Kings were the founders of the Three Dynasties, the Hsia, the Shang, and the Chou.

rejoice in life nor look on death as a calamity, for it knows that no fixed rule can be assigned to beginning and end.

"Calculate what man knows and it cannot compare to what he does not know. Calculate the time he is alive and it cannot compare to the time before he was born. Yet man takes something so small and tries to exhaust the dimensions of something so large! Hence he is muddled and confused and can never get anywhere. Looking at it this way, how do we know that the tip of a hair can be singled out as the measure of the smallest thing possible? Or how do we know that heaven and earth can fully encompass the dimensions of the largest thing possible?"

The Lord of the River said, "Men who debate such matters these days all claim that the minutest thing has no form and the largest thing cannot be encompassed. Is this a true statement?"

Jo of the North Sea said, "If from the standpoint of the minute we look at what is large, we cannot see to the end. If from the standpoint of what is large we look at what is minute, we cannot distinguish it clearly. The minute is the smallest of the small, the gigantic is the largest of the large, and it is therefore convenient to distinguish between them. But this is merely a matter of circumstance. Before we can speak of coarse or fine, however, there must be some form. If a thing has no form, then numbers cannot express its dimensions, and if it cannot be encompassed, then numbers cannot express its size. We can use words to talk about the coarseness of things and we can use our minds to visualize the fineness of things. But what words cannot describe and the mind cannot succeed in visualizing—this has nothing to do with coarseness or fineness.

"Therefore the Great Man in his actions will not harm others, but he makes no show of benevolence or charity. He will not move for the sake of profit, but he does not despise the porter at the gate. He will not wrangle for goods or wealth, but he makes no show of refusing or relinquishing them. He will not enlist the help of others in his work, but he makes no show of being self-supporting, and he does not despise the greedy and base. His actions differ from those of the mob, but he makes no show of uniqueness or eccentricity. He is content to stay behind with the crowd, but he does not despise those who run forward to flatter and fawn. All the titles and stipends of the age are not enough to stir him to exertion; all its penalties and censures are not enough to make him feel shame. He knows that no line can be drawn between right and wrong, no border can be fixed between great and small. I have heard it said, 'The Man of the Way wins no fame, the highest virtue[8] wins no gain, the Great Man has no self.' To the most perfect degree, he goes along with what has been alloted to him."

The Lord of the River said, "Whether they are external to things or internal, I do not understand how we come to have these distinctions of noble and mean or of great and small."

Jo of the North Sea said, "From the point of view of the Way, things have no nobility or meanness. From the point of view of things themselves, each regards itself as noble and other things as mean. From the point of view of common opinion, nobility and meanness are not determined by the individual himself.

"From the point of view of differences, if we regard a thing as big because there is a certain bigness to it, then among all the ten thousand things there are none that are not big. If we regard a thing as small because there is a certain smallness to it, then among the ten thousand things there are none that are not small. If we know that heaven and earth are tiny grains

---

[8] A play on the homophones *te* (virtue) and *te* (gain, or acquisition).

and the tip of a hair is a range of mountains, then we have perceived the law of difference.

"From the point of view of function, if we regard a thing as useful because there is a certain usefulness to it, then among all the ten thousand things there are none that are not useful. If we regard a thing as useless because there is a certain uselessness to it, then among the ten thousand things there are none that are not useless. If we know that east and west are mutually opposed but that one cannot do without the other, then we can estimate the degree of function.

"From the point of view of preference, if we regard a thing as right because there is a certain right to it, then among the ten thousand things there are none that are not right. If we regard a thing as wrong because there is a certain wrong to it, then among the ten thousand things there are none that are not wrong. If we know that Yao and Chieh each thought himself right and condemned the other as wrong, then we may understand how there are preferences in behavior.

"In ancient times Yao abdicated in favor of Shun and Shun ruled as emperor; K'uai abdicated in favor of Chih and Chih was destroyed.[9] T'ang and Wu fought and became kings; Duke Po fought and was wiped out.[10] Looking at it this way, we see that struggling or giving way, behaving like a Yao or like a Chieh, may be at one time noble and at another time mean. It is impossible to establish any constant rule.

"A beam or pillar can be used to batter down a city wall, but

[9] In 316 B.C. King K'uai of Yen was persuaded to imitate the example of Yao by ceding his throne to his minister Tzu Chih. In no time the state was torn by internal strife and three years later it was invaded and annexed by the state of Ch'i.

[10] T'ang and Wu were the founders of the Shang and Chou dynasties respectively. Duke Po was a scion of the royal family of Ch'u who led an unsuccessful revolt against its ruler and was defeated and forced to commit suicide in 479 B.C.

it is no good for stopping up a little hole—this refers to a difference in function. Thoroughbreds like Ch'i-chi and Hua-liu could gallop a thousand li in one day, but when it came to catching rats they were no match for the wildcat or the weasel —this refers to a difference in skill. The horned owl catches fleas at night and can spot the tip of a hair, but when daylight comes, no matter how wide it opens its eyes, it cannot see a mound or a hill—this refers to a difference in nature. Now do you say that you are going to make Right your master and do away with Wrong, or make Order your master and do away with Disorder? If you do, then you have not understood the principle of heaven and earth or the nature of the ten thousand things. This is like saying that you are going to make Heaven your master and do away with Earth, or make Yin your master and do away with Yang. Obviously it is impossible. If men persist in talking this way without stop, they must be either fools or deceivers!

"Emperors and kings have different ways of ceding their thrones; the Three Dynasties had different rules of succession. Those who went against the times and flouted custom were called usurpers; those who went with the times and followed custom were called companions of righteousness. Be quiet, be quiet, O Lord of the River! How could you understand anything about the gateway of nobility and meanness or the house of great and small?"

"Well then," said the Lord of the River, "what should I do and what should I not do? How am I to know in the end what to accept and what to reject, what to abide by and what to discard?"

Jo of the North Sea said, "From the point of view of the Way, what is noble or what is mean? These are merely what are called endless changes. Do not hobble your will, or you will be departing far from the Way! What is few, or what is many? These are merely what are called boundless turnings.[11] Do not strive to unify your actions, or you will be at sixes and sevens with the Way! Be stern like the ruler of a state—he grants no private favor. Be benign and impartial like the god of the soil at the sacrifice—he grants no private blessing. Be broad and expansive like the endlessness of the four directions—they have nothing which bounds or hedges them. Embrace the ten thousand things universally—how could there be one you should give special support to? This is called being without bent. When the ten thousand things are unified and equal, then which is short and which is long?

"The Way is without beginning or end, but things have their life and death—you cannot rely upon their fulfillment. One moment empty, the next moment full—you cannot depend upon their form. The years cannot be held off; time cannot be stopped. Decay, growth, fullness, and emptiness end and then begin again. It is thus that we must describe the plan of the Great Meaning and discuss the principles of the ten thousand things. The life of things is a gallop, a headlong dash—with every movement they alter, with every moment they shift. What should you do and what should you not do? Everything will change of itself, that is certain!"

"If that is so," said the Lord of the River, "then what is there valuable about the Way?"

Jo of the North Sea said, "He who understands the Way is certain to have command of basic principles. He who has com-

---

[11] I follow Fukunaga's interpretation of these terms.

mand of basic principles is certain to know how to deal with circumstances. And he who knows how to deal with circumstances will not allow things to do him harm. When a man has perfect virtue, fire cannot burn him, water cannot drown him, cold and heat cannot afflict him, birds and beasts cannot injure him. I do not say that he makes light of these things. I mean that he distinguishes between safety and danger, contents himself with fortune or misfortune, and is cautious in his comings and goings. Therefore nothing can harm him.

"Hence it is said: the Heavenly is on the inside, the human is on the outside. Virtue resides in the Heavenly. Understand the actions of Heaven and man, base yourself upon Heaven, take your stand in virtue,[12] and then, although you hasten or hold back, bend or stretch, you may return to the essential and speak of the ultimate."

"What do you mean by the Heavenly and the human?"

Jo of the North Sea said, "Horses and oxen have four feet—this is what I mean by the Heavenly. Putting a halter on the horse's head, piercing the ox's nose—this is what I mean by the human. So I say: do not let what is human wipe out what is Heavenly; do not let what is purposeful wipe out what is fated; do not let [the desire for] gain lead you after fame. Be cautious, guard it, and do not lose it—this is what I mean by returning to the True."

The K'uei[13] envies the millepede, the millepede envies the snake, the snake envies the wind, the wind envies the eye, and the eye envies the mind.

[12] Actually, the text reads "gain" (*te*); perhaps this is merely a mistake for the *te* meaning "virtue," or perhaps a play on the two words is intended. See above, p. 100, n. 8.

[13] A being with only one leg. Sometimes it is described as a spirit or a strange beast, sometimes as a historical personage—the Music Master K'uei.

The K'uei said to the millepede, "I have this one leg that I hop along on, though I make little progress. Now how in the world do you manage to work all those ten thousand legs of yours?"

The millepede said, "You don't understand. Haven't you ever watched a man spit? He just gives a hawk and out it comes, some drops as big as pearls, some as fine as mist, raining down in a jumble of countless particles. Now all I do is put in motion the heavenly mechanism in me—I'm not aware of how the thing works."

The millepede said to the snake, "I have all these legs that I move along on, but I can't seem to keep up with you who have no legs. How is that?"

The snake said, "It's just the heavenly mechanism moving me along—how can I change the way I am? What would I do with legs if I had them?"

The snake said to the wind, "I move my backbone and ribs and manage to get along, though I still have some kind of body. But now you come whirling up from the North Sea and go whirling off to the South Sea, and you don't seem to have any body. How is that?"

The wind said, "It's true that I whirl up from the North Sea and whirl off to the South Sea. But if you hold up a finger against me you've defeated me, and if you trample on me you've likewise defeated me. On the other hand, I can break down big trees and blow over great houses—this is a talent that I alone have. So I take all the mass of little defeats and make them into a Great Victory. To make a Great Victory —only the sage is capable of that!"

When Confucius was passing through K'uang, the men of Sung surrounded him with several encirclements of troops, but he went right on playing his lute and singing without a stop.[14] Tzu Lu went in to see him and said, "Master, how can you be so carefree?"

Confucius said, "Come, I will explain to you. For a long time I have tried to stay out of the way of hardship. That I have not managed to escape it is due to fate. For a long time I have tried to achieve success. That I have not been able to do so is due to the times. If it happens to be the age of a Yao or a Shun, then there are no men in the world who face hardship—but this is not because their wisdom saves them. If it happens to be the age of a Chieh or a Chou, then there are no men in the world who achieve success—but this is not because their wisdom fails them. It is time and circumstance that make it so.

"To travel across the water without shrinking from the sea serpent or the dragon—this is the courage of the fisherman. To travel over land without shrinking from the rhinoceros or the tiger—this is the courage of the hunter. To see the bare blades clashing before him and to look upon death as though it were life—this is the courage of the man of ardor.[15] To understand that hardship is a matter of fate, that success is a matter of the times, and to face great difficulty without fear—this is the courage of the sage. Be content with it, Tzu Lu. My fate has been decided for me."

Shortly afterwards the leader of the armed men came forward and apologized. "We thought you were Yang Huo and

[14] The *Analects* twice states (IX, 5; XI, 22): "The Master was put in fear in K'uang." It is said that the people of the state in which K'uang was situated, here identified as Sung, mistook Confucius for an enemy of theirs named Yang Huo.

[15] A man who is willing to sacrifice his life to save others or to preserve his honor.

that was why we surrounded you. Now that we see you aren't, we beg to take leave and withdraw."

Kung-sun Lung said to Prince Mou of Wei,[16] "When I was young I studied the Way of the former kings, and when I grew older I came to understand the conduct of benevolence and righteousness. I reconciled difference and sameness, distinguished hardness and whiteness, and proved that not so was so, that the unacceptable was acceptable. I confounded the wisdom of the hundred schools and demolished the arguments of a host of speakers. I believed that I had attained the highest degree of accomplishment. But now I have heard the words of Chuang Tzu and I am bewildered by their strangeness. I don't know whether my arguments are not as good as his, or whether I am no match for him in understanding. I find now that I can't even open my beak. May I ask what you advise?"

Prince Mou leaned on his armrest and gave a great sigh, and then he looked up at the sky and laughed, saying, "Haven't you ever heard about the frog in the caved-in well? He said to the great turtle of the Eastern Sea, 'What fun I have! I come out and hop around the railing of the well, or I go back in and take a rest in the wall where a tile has fallen out. When I dive into the water, I let it hold me up under the armpits and support my chin, and when I slip about in the mud, I bury my feet in it and let it come up over my ankles. I look around at the mosquito larvae and the crabs and polli-

[16] The logician Kung-sun Lung, who spent much time discussing the concepts of sameness and difference or the relationship of attributes such as hardness and whiteness to the thing they qualify, has already been referred to; see p. 35, n. 7, and p. 37, n. 9. Prince Mou of Wei was the reputed author of a Taoist work in four sections which is no longer extant.

wogs and I see that none of them can match me. To have complete command of the water of one whole valley and to monopolize all the joys of a caved-in well—this is the best there is! Why don't you come some time and see for yourself?'

"But before the great turtle of the Eastern Sea had even gotten his left foot in the well his right knee was already wedged fast. He backed out and withdrew a little, and then began to describe the sea. 'A distance of a thousand li cannot indicate its greatness; a depth of a thousand fathoms cannot express how deep it is. In the time of Yü there were floods for nine years out of ten, and yet its waters never rose. In the time of T'ang there were droughts for seven years out of eight, and yet its shores never receded. Never to alter or shift, whether for an instant or an eternity; never to advance or recede, whether the quantity of water flowing in is great or small—this is the great delight of the Eastern Sea!'

"When the frog in the caved-in well heard this, he was dumfounded with surprise, crestfallen, and completely at a loss. Now your knowledge cannot even define the borders of right and wrong, and still you try to see through the words of Chuang Tzu—this is like trying to make a mosquito carry a mountain on its back or a pill bug race across the Yellow River. You will never be up to the task!

He whose understanding cannot grasp these minute and subtle words, but is only fit to win some temporary gain—is he not like the frog in the caved-in well? Chuang Tzu, now—at this very moment he is treading the Yellow Springs[17] or leaping up to the vast blue. To him there is no north or south—in utter freedom he dissolves himself in the four directions and drowns himself in the unfathomable. To him there is no east or west—he begins in the Dark Obscu-

---

[17] The underworld.

rity and returns to the Great Thoroughfare. Now you come niggling along and try to spy him out or fix some name to him, but this is like using a tube to scan the sky or an awl to measure the depth of the earth—the instrument is too small, is it not? You'd better be on your way! Or perhaps you've never heard about the young boy of Shou-ling who went to learn the Han-tan Walk. He hadn't mastered what the Han-tan people had to teach him when he forgot his old way of walking, so that he had to crawl all the way back home. Now if you don't get on your way, you're likely to forget what you knew before and be out of a job!"

Kung-sun Lung's mouth fell open and wouldn't stay closed. His tongue stuck to the roof of his mouth and wouldn't come down. In the end he broke into a run and fled.

Once, when Chuang Tzu was fishing in the P'u River, the king of Ch'u sent two officials to go and announce to him: "I would like to trouble you with the administration of my realm."

Chuang Tzu held on to the fishing pole and, without turning his head, said, "I have heard that there is a sacred tortoise in Ch'u that has been dead for three thousand years. The king keeps it wrapped in cloth and boxed, and stores it in the ancestral temple. Now would this tortoise rather be dead and have its bones left behind and honored? Or would it rather be alive and dragging its tail in the mud?"

"It would rather be alive and dragging its tail in the mud," said the two officials.

Chuang Tzu said, "Go away! I'll drag my tail in the mud!"

When Hui Tzu was prime minister of Liang, Chuang Tzu set off to visit him. Someone said to Hui Tzu, "Chuang Tzu is coming because he wants to replace you as prime minister!" With this Hui Tzu was filled with alarm and searched all over the state for three days and three nights trying to find Chuang Tzu. Chuang Tzu then came to see him and said, "In the south there is a bird called the Yüan-ch'u—I wonder if you've ever heard of it? The Yüan-ch'u rises up from the South Sea and flies to the North Sea, and it will rest on nothing but the Wu-t'ung tree, eat nothing but the fruit of the Lien, and drink only from springs of sweet water. Once there was an owl who had gotten hold of a half-rotten old rat, and as the Yüan-ch'u passed by, it raised its head, looked up at the Yüan-ch'u, and said, 'Shoo!' Now that you have this Liang state of yours, are you trying to shoo me?"

Chuang Tzu and Hui Tzu were strolling along the dam of the Hao River when Chuang Tzu said, "See how the minnows come out and dart around where they please! That's what fish really enjoy!"

Hui Tzu said, "You're not a fish—how do you know what fish enjoy?"

Chuang Tzu said, "You're not I, so how do you know I don't know what fish enjoy?"

Hui Tzu said, "I'm not you, so I certainly don't know what you know. On the other hand, you're certainly not a fish—so that still proves you don't know what fish enjoy!"

Chuang Tzu said, "Let's go back to your original question, please. You asked me *how* I know what fish enjoy—so you already knew I knew it when you asked the question. I know it by standing here beside the Hao."

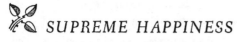 *SUPREME HAPPINESS*

(SECTION 18)

Is there such a thing as supreme happiness in the world or isn't there? Is there some way to keep yourself alive or isn't there? What to do, what to rely on, what to avoid, what to stick by, what to follow, what to leave alone, what to find happiness in, what to hate?

This is what the world honors: wealth, eminence, long life, a good name. This is what the world finds happiness in: a life of ease, rich food, fine clothes, beautiful sights, sweet sounds. This is what it looks down on: poverty, meanness, early death, a bad name. This is what it finds bitter: a life that knows no rest, a mouth that gets no rich food, no fine clothes for the body, no beautiful sights for the eye, no sweet sounds for the ear.

People who can't get these things fret a great deal and are afraid—this is a stupid way to treat the body. People who are rich wear themselves out rushing around on business, piling up more wealth than they could ever use—this is a superficial way to treat the body. People who are eminent spend night and day scheming and wondering if they are doing right— this is a shoddy way to treat the body. Man lives his life in company with worry, and if he lives a long while, till he's dull and doddering, then he has spent that much time worrying instead of dying, a bitter lot indeed! This is a callous way to treat the body.

Men of ardor[1] are regarded by the world as good, but their goodness doesn't succeed in keeping them alive. So I don't know whether their goodness is really good or not. Perhaps I think it's good—but not good enough to save their lives. Perhaps I think it's no good—but still good enough to save the lives of others. So I say, if your loyal advice isn't heeded, give way and do not wrangle. Tzu-hsü wrangled and lost his body.[2] But if he hadn't wrangled, he wouldn't have made a name. Is there really such a thing as goodness or isn't there?

What ordinary people do and what they find happiness in —I don't know whether such happiness is in the end really happiness or not. I look at what ordinary people find happiness in, what they all make a mad dash for, racing around as though they couldn't stop—they all say they're happy with it. I'm not happy with it and I'm not unhappy with it. In the end is there really happiness or isn't there?

I take inaction to be true happiness, but ordinary people think it is a bitter thing. I say: the highest happiness has no happiness, the highest praise has no praise. The world can't decide what is right and what is wrong. And yet inaction can decide this. The highest happiness, keeping alive—only inaction gets you close to this!

Let me try putting it this way. The inaction of Heaven is its purity, the inaction of earth is its peace. So the two inactions combine and all things are transformed and brought to birth. Wonderfully, mysteriously, there is no place they come out of. Mysteriously, wonderfully, they have no sign. Each thing minds its business and all grow up out of inaction. So

[1] See above, p. 106, n. 15.
[2] Wu Tzu-hsü, minister to the king of Wu, repeatedly warned the king of the danger of attack from the state of Yüeh. He finally aroused the king's ire and suspicion and was forced to commit suicide in 484 B.C.

I say, Heaven and earth do nothing and there is nothing that is not done. Among men, who can get hold of this inaction?

Chuang Tzu's wife died. When Hui Tzu went to convey his condolences, he found Chuang Tzu sitting with his legs sprawled out, pounding on a tub and singing. "You lived with her, she brought up your children and grew old," said Hui Tzu. "It should be enough simply not to weep at her death. But pounding on a tub and singing—this is going too far, isn't it?"

Chuang Tzu said, "You're wrong. When she first died, do you think I didn't grieve like anyone else? But I looked back to her beginning and the time before she was born. Not only the time before she was born, but the time before she had a body. Not only the time before she had a body, but the time before she had a spirit. In the midst of the jumble of wonder and mystery a change took place and she had a spirit. Another change and she had a body. Another change and she was born. Now there's been another change and she's dead. It's just like the progression of the four seasons, spring, summer, fall, winter.

"Now she's going to lie down peacefully in a vast room. If I were to follow after her bawling and sobbing, it would show that I don't understand anything about fate. So I stopped."

Uncle Lack-Limb and Uncle Lame-Gait were seeing the sights at Dark Lord Hill and the wastes of K'un-lun, the place where the Yellow Emperor rested.[3] Suddenly a willow

---

[3] These are all places or persons associated in Chinese legend with immortality. The Yellow Emperor, as we have seen above, p. 78, did not die but ascended to Heaven.

sprouted out of Uncle Lame-Gait's left elbow.[4] He looked very startled and seemed to be annoyed.

"Do you resent it?" said Uncle Lack-Limb.

"No—what is there to resent?" said Uncle Lame-Gait. "To live is to borrow. And if we borrow to live, then life must be a pile of trash. Life and death are day and night. You and I came to watch the process of change, and now change has caught up with me. Why would I have anything to resent?"

When Chuang Tzu went to Ch'u, he saw an old skull, all dry and parched. He poked it with his carriage whip and then asked, "Sir, were you greedy for life and forgetful of reason, and so came to this? Was your state overthrown and did you bow beneath the ax and so came to this? Did you do some evil deed and were you ashamed to bring disgrace upon your parents and family, and so came to this? Was it through the pangs of cold and hunger that you came to this? Or did your springs and autumns pile up until they brought you to this?"

When he had finished speaking, he dragged the skull over and, using it for a pillow, lay down to sleep.

In the middle of the night, the skull came to him in a dream and said, "You chatter like a rhetorician and all your words betray the entanglements of a living man. The dead know nothing of these! Would you like to hear a lecture on the dead?"

"Indeed," said Chuang Tzu.

The skull said, "Among the dead there are no rulers above, no subjects below, and no chores of the four seasons. With nothing to do, our springs and autumns are as endless as

[4] According to the more prosaic interpretation of Li Tz'u-ming, the character for "willow" is a loan for the word "tumor."

heaven and earth. A king facing south on his throne could have no more happiness than this!"

Chuang Tzu couldn't believe this and said, "If I got the Arbiter of Fate to give you a body again, make you some bones and flesh, return you to your parents and family and your old home and friends, you would want that, wouldn't you?"

The skull frowned severely, wrinkling up its brow. "Why would I throw away more happiness than that of a king on a throne and take on the troubles of a human being again?" it said.

When Yen Yüan went east to Ch'i, Confucius had a very worried look on his face.[5] Tzu-kung got off his mat and asked, "May I be so bold as to inquire why the Master has such a worried expression now that Hui has gone east to Ch'i?"

"Excellent—this question of yours," said Confucius. "Kuan Tzu[6] had a saying that I much approve of: 'Small bags won't hold big things; short well ropes won't dip up deep water.' In the same way I believe that fate has certain forms and the body certain appropriate uses. You can't add to or take away from these. I'm afraid that when Hui gets to Ch'i he will start telling the marquis of Ch'i about the ways of Yao, Shun, and the Yellow Emperor, and then will go on to speak about Sui-jen and Shen-nung.[7] The marquis will then look for similar greatness within himself and fail to find it. Failing to find it, he will become distraught, and when a man becomes distraught, he kills.

[5] Yen Yüan or Yen Hui, who has appeared earlier, was Confucius' favorite disciple.

[6] Kuan Chung, a 7th-century statesman of Ch'i whom Confucius, judging from the *Analects*, admired.

[7] Sui-jen and Shen-nung are mythical culture heroes, the discoverers of fire and agriculture respectively.

"Haven't you heard this story? Once a sea bird alighted in the suburbs of the Lu capital. The marquis of Lu escorted it to the ancestral temple, where he entertained it, performing the Nine Shao music for it to listen to and presenting it with the meat of the T'ai-lao sacrifice to feast on. But the bird only looked dazed and forlorn, refusing to eat a single slice of meat or drink a cup of wine, and in three days it was dead. This is to try to nourish a bird with what would nourish you instead of what would nourish a bird. If you want to nourish a bird with what nourishes a bird, then you should let it roost in the deep forest, play among the banks and islands, float on the rivers and lakes, eat mudfish and minnows, follow the rest of the flock in flight and rest, and live any way it chooses. A bird hates to hear even the sound of human voices, much less all that hubbub and to-do. Try performing the Hsien-ch'ih and Nine Shao music in the wilds around Lake Tung-t'ing—when the birds hear it they will fly off, when the animals hear it they will run away, when the fish hear it they will dive to the bottom. Only the people who hear it will gather around to listen. Fish live in water and thrive, but if men tried to live in water they would die. Creatures differ because they have different likes and dislikes. Therefore the former sages never required the same ability from all creatures or made them all do the same thing. Names should stop when they have expressed reality, concepts of right should be founded on what is suitable. This is what it means to have command of reason, and good fortune to support you."

Lieh Tzu was on a trip and was eating by the roadside when he saw a hundred-year-old skull. Pulling away the weeds and pointing his finger, he said, "Only you and I know that you have never died and you have never lived. Are you really unhappy? [8] Am I really enjoying myself?"

The seeds of things have mysterious workings. In the water they become Break Vine, on the edges of the water they become Frog's Robe. If they sprout on the slopes they become Hill Slippers. If Hill Slippers get rich soil, they turn into Crow's Feet. The roots of Crow's Feet turn into maggots and their leaves turn into butterflies. Before long the butterflies are transformed and turn into insects that live under the stove; they look like snakes and their name is Ch'ü-t'o. After a thousand days, the Ch'ü-t'o insects become birds called Dried Leftover Bones. The saliva of the Dried Leftover Bones becomes Ssu-mi bugs and the Ssu-mi bugs become Vinegar Eaters. Yi-lo bugs are born from the Vinegar Eaters, and Huang-shuang bugs from Chiu-yu bugs. Chiu-yu bugs are born from Mou-jui bugs and Mou-jui bugs are born from Rot Grubs and Rot Grubs are born from Sheep's Groom. Sheep's Groom couples with bamboo that has not sprouted for a long while and produces Green Peace plants. Green Peace plants produce leopards and leopards produce horses and horses produce men. Men in time return again to the mysterious workings. So all creatures come out of the mysterious workings and go back into them again. [9]

[8] Following the interpretation of Yü Yüeh.
[9] The text of this last paragraph, a romp through ancient Chinese nature lore, is doubtful at many points.

 *MASTERING LIFE*

(SECTION 19)

He who has mastered the true nature of life does not labor over what life cannot do. He who has mastered the true nature of fate does not labor over what knowledge cannot change. He who wants to nourish his body must first of all turn to things. And yet it is possible to have more than enough things and for the body still to go unnourished. He who has life must first of all see to it that it does not leave the body. And yet it is possible for life never to leave the body and still fail to be preserved. The coming of life cannot be fended off, its departure cannot be stopped. How pitiful the men of the world, who think that simply nourishing the body is enough to preserve life! Then why is what the world does worth doing? It may not be worth doing, and yet it cannot be left undone—this is unavoidable.

He who wants to avoid doing anything for his body had best abandon the world. By abandoning the world, he can be without entanglements. Being without entanglements, he can be upright and calm. Being upright and calm, he can be born again with others. Being born again, he can come close [to the Way].

But why is abandoning the affairs of the world worth while, and why is forgetting life worth while? If you abandon the affairs of the world, your body will be without toil. If you forget life, your vitality will be unimpaired. With your body complete and your vitality made whole again, you may become one with Heaven. Heaven and earth are the father and mother of the ten thousand things. They join to become a body; they part to become a beginning. When the body and vitality are without flaw, this is called being able to shift. Vitality added to vitality, you return to become the Helper of Heaven.

Master Lieh Tzu said to the Barrier Keeper Yin, "The Perfect Man can walk under water without choking, can tread on fire without being burned, and can travel above the ten thousand things without being frightened. May I ask how he manages this?"

The Barrier Keeper Yin replied, "This is because he guards the pure breath—it has nothing to do with wisdom, skill, determination, or courage. Sit down and I will tell you about it. All that have faces, forms, voices, colors—these are all mere things. How could one thing and another thing be far removed from each other? And how could any of them be worth considering as a predecessor? They are forms, colors—nothing more. But things have their creation in what has no form, and their conclusion in what has no change. If a man can get hold of *this* and exhaust it fully, then how can things stand in his way? He may rest within the bounds that know no excess, hide within the borders that know no source, wander where the ten thousand things have their end and beginning, unify his nature, nourish his breath, unite his virtue, and thereby communicate with that which creates all things. A man like this guards what belongs to Heaven and keeps it whole. His spirit has no flaw, so how can things enter in and get at him?

"When a drunken man falls from a carriage, though the carriage may be going very fast, he won't be killed. He has bones and joints the same as other men, and yet he is not injured as they would be, because his spirit is whole. He didn't know he was riding, and he doesn't know he has fallen out. Life and death, alarm and terror do not enter his breast, and so he can bang against things without fear of injury. If he can keep himself whole like this by means of wine, how much more can he keep himself whole by means of Heaven! The sage hides himself in Heaven—hence there is nothing that can do him harm.

"A man seeking revenge does not go so far as to smash the sword of his enemy; a man, no matter how hot-tempered, does not rail at the tile that happens to fall on him. To know that all things in the world are equal and the same—this is the only way to eliminate the chaos of attack and battle and the harshness of punishment and execution!

"Do not try to develop what is natural to man; develop what is natural to Heaven. He who develops Heaven benefits life; he who develops man injures life. Do not reject what is of Heaven, do not neglect what is of man, and the people will be close to the attainment of Truth." [1]

When Confucius was on his way to Ch'u, he passed through a forest where he saw a hunchback catching cicadas with a sticky pole as easily as though he were grabbing them with his hand.

Confucius said, "What skill you have! Is there a special way to this?"

"I have a way," said the hunchback. "For the first five or six months I practice balancing two balls on top of each other on the end of the pole and, if they don't fall off, I know I will

---

[1] I follow the text as it stands, though it would perhaps be preferable to adopt Ma Hsü-lun's suggestion, dropping the *min* and translating "and you will be close to the attainment of Truth."

lose very few cicadas. Then I balance three balls and, if they don't fall off, I know I'll lose only one cicada in ten. Then I balance five balls and, if they don't fall off, I know it will be as easy as grabbing them with my hand. I hold my body like a stiff tree trunk and use my arm like an old dry limb. No matter how huge heaven and earth, or how numerous the ten thousand things, I'm aware of nothing but cicada wings. Not wavering, not tipping, not letting any of the other ten thousand things take the place of those cicada wings—how can I help but succeed?"

Confucius turned to his disciples and said, "He keeps his will undivided and concentrates his spirit—that would serve to describe our hunchback gentleman here, would it not?"

Yen Yüan said to Confucius, "I once crossed the gulf at Goblet Deeps and the ferryman handled the boat with supernatural skill. I asked him, 'Can a person learn how to handle a boat?' and he replied, 'Certainly. A good swimmer will get the knack of it in no time. And, if a man can swim under water, he may never have seen a boat before and still he'll know how to handle it!' I asked him what he meant by that, but he wouldn't tell me. May I venture to ask you what it means?"

Confucius said, "A good swimmer will get the knack of it in no time—that means he's forgotten the water. If a man can swim under water, he may never have seen a boat before and still he'll know how to handle it—that's because he sees the water as so much dry land, and regards the capsizing of a boat as he would the overturning of a cart. The ten thousand things[2] may all be capsizing and turning over at the

[2] Following the interpretation of Yü Yüeh, who supplies a *wu* after the *wan*.

same time right in from of him and it can't get at him and affect what's inside—so where could he go and not be at ease?

"When you're betting for tiles in an archery contest, you shoot with skill. When you're betting for fancy belt buckles, you worry about your aim. And when you're betting for real gold, you're a nervous wreck. Your skill is the same in all three cases—but because one prize means more to you than another, you let outside considerations weigh on your mind. He who looks too hard at the outside gets clumsy on the inside."

T'ien K'ai-chih went to see Duke Wei of Chou. Duke Wei said, "I hear that Chu Hsien is studying how to live. You are a friend of his—what have you heard from him on the subject?"

T'ien K'ai-chih said, "I merely wield a broom and tend his gate and garden—how should I have heard anything from the Master?"

Duke Wei said, "Don't be modest, Master T'ien. I am ·anxious to hear about it."

T'ien K'ai-chih said, "I have heard the Master say, 'He who is good at nourishing life is like a herder of sheep—he watches for stragglers and whips them up.' "

"What does that mean?" asked Duke Wei.

T'ien K'ai-chih said, "In Lu there was Shan Pao—he lived among the cliffs, drank only water, and didn't go after gain like other people. He went along like that for seventy years and still had the complexion of a little child. Unfortunately, he met a hungry tiger who killed him and ate him up. Then there was Chang Yi—there wasn't one of the great families and fancy mansions that he didn't rush off to visit. He went along like that for forty years, and then he developed an internal fever, fell ill, and died. Shan Pao looked after what was on the inside and the tiger ate up his outside. Chang Yi looked after what was on the outside and the sickness attacked him from the inside. Both these men failed to give a lash to the stragglers." [8]

Confucius has said, "Don't go in and hide; don't come out and shine; stand stock-still in the middle." He who can follow these three rules is sure to be called the finest. When people are worried about the safety of the roads, if they hear that one traveler in a party of ten has been murdered, then fathers and sons, elder and younger brothers will warn each other to be careful and will not venture out until they have a large escort of armed men. That's wise of them, isn't it? But when it comes to what people really ought to be worried about—the time when they are lying in bed or sitting around eating and drinking—then they don't have sense enough to take warning. That's a mistake!"

The Invocator of the Ancestors, dressed in his black, square-cut robes, peered into the pigpen and said, "Why should you object to dying? I'm going to fatten you for three months, practice austerities for ten days, fast for three days, spread the white rushes, and lay your shoulders and rump on the carved sacrificial stand—you'll go along with that, won't you? True, if I were planning things from the point of view of a pig, I'd say is would be better to eat chaff and bran and stay right there in the pen. But if I were planning for myself, I'd say that if I could be honored as a high official while I lived, and get to ride in a fine hearse and lie among the feathers and trappings

[8] That is, stick to a happy medium.

when I died, I'd go along with that. Speaking for the pig, I'd give such a life a flat refusal, but speaking for myself, I'd certainly accept. I wonder why I look at things differently from a pig?"

Duke Huan was hunting in a marsh, with Kuan Chung as his carriage driver, when he saw a ghost. The duke grasped Kuan Chung's hand and said, "Father Chung, what do you see?" [4]

"I don't see anything," replied Kuan Chung.

When the duke returned home, he fell into a stupor, grew ill, and for several days did not go out.

A gentleman of Ch'i named Huang-tzu Kao-ao said, "Your Grace, you are doing this injury to yourself! How could a ghost have the power to injure you! If the vital breath that is stored up in a man becomes dispersed and does not return, then he suffers a deficiency. If it ascends and fails to descend again, it causes him to be chronically irritable. If it descends and does not ascend again, it causes him to be chronically forgetful. And if it neither ascends nor descends, but gathers in the middle of the body in the region of the heart, then he becomes ill."

Duke Huan said, "But do ghosts really exist?"

"Indeed they do. There is the Li on the hearth [5] and the Chi in the stove. The heap of clutter and trash just inside the gate is where the Lei-t'ing lives. In the northeast corner the Pei-a and Kuei-lung leap about, and the northwest corner is

[4] Duke Huan of Ch'i (r. 685–643 B.C.) later became the first of the *pa*— dictators or hegemons who imposed their will upon the other feudal lords. Kuan Chung (d. 645 B.C.) was his chief minister. As a special mark of esteem, the duke customarily addressed him as "Father Chung."

[5] Following the emendation and interpretation of Yü Yüeh.

where the Yi-yang lives. In the water is the Kang-hsiang; on the hills, the Hsin; in the mountains, the K'uei;[6] in the meadows, the P'ang-huang; and in the marshes, the Wei-t'o."

The duke said, "May I ask what a Wei-t'o looks like?"

Huang-tzu said, "The Wei-t'o is as big as a wheel hub, as tall as a carriage shaft, has a purple robe and a vermilion hat and, as creatures go, is very ugly. When it hears the sound of thunder or a carriage, it grabs its head and stands up. Anyone who sees it will soon become a dictator."

Duke Huan's face lit up and he said with a laugh, "*That* must have been what I saw!" Then he straightened his robe and hat and sat up on the mat with Huang-tzu, and before the day was over, though he didn't notice it, his illness went away.

Chi Hsing-tzu was training gamecocks for the king. After ten days the king asked if they were ready.

"Not yet. They're too haughty and rely on their nerve."

Another ten days and the king asked again.

"Not yet. They still respond to noises and movements."

Another ten days and the king asked again.

"Not yet. They still look around fiercely and are full of spirit."

Another ten days and the king asked again.

"They're close enough. Another cock can crow and they show no sign of change. Look at them from a distance and you'd think they were made of wood. Their virtue is complete. Other cocks won't dare face up to them, but will turn and run."

* The one-legged creature who has already appeared above, on p. 104.

Confucius was seeing the sights at Lü-liang, where the water falls from a height of thirty fathoms and races and boils along for forty li, so swift that no fish or other water creature can swim in it. He saw a man dive into the water and, supposing that the man was in some kind of trouble and intended to end his life, he ordered his disciples to line up on the bank and pull the man out. But after the man had gone a couple of hundred paces, he came out of the water and began strolling along the base of the embankment, his hair streaming down, singing a song. Confucius ran after him and said, "At first I thought you were a ghost, but now I see you're a man. May I ask if you have some special way of staying afloat in the water?"

"I have no way. I began with what I was used to, grew up with my nature, and let things come to completion with fate. I go under with the swirls and come out with the eddies, following along the way the water goes and never thinking about myself. That's how I can stay afloat."

Confucius said, "What do you mean by saying that you began with what you were used to, grew up with your nature, and let things come to completion with fate?"

"I was born on the dry land and felt safe on the dry land— that was what I was used to. I grew up with the water and felt safe in the water—that was my nature. I don't know why I do what I do—that's fate."

Woodworker Ch'ing[7] carved a piece of wood and made a bell stand, and when it was finished, everyone who saw it marveled, for it seemed to be the work of gods or spirits. When

[7] A carpenter of Lu, mentioned in the *Tso chuan* under Duke Hsiang, 4th year (569 B.C).

the marquis of Lu saw it, he asked, "What art is it you have?"

Ch'ing replied, "I am only a craftsman—how would I have any art? There is one thing, however. When I am going to make a bell stand, I never let it wear out my energy. I always fast in order to still my mind. When I have fasted for three days, I no longer have any thought of congratulations or rewards, of titles or stipends. When I have fasted for five days, I no longer have any thought of praise or blame, of skill or clumsiness. And when I have fasted for seven days, I am so still that I forget I have four limbs and a form and body. By that time, the ruler and his court no longer exist for me. My skill is concentrated and all outside distractions fade away. After that, I go into the mountain forest and examine the Heavenly nature of the trees. If I find one of superlative form, and I can see a bell stand there, I put my hand to the job of carving; if not, I let it go. This way I am simply matching up 'Heaven' with 'Heaven.' [8] That's probably the reason that people wonder if the results were not made by spirits."

Tung-yeh Chi was displaying his carriage driving before Duke Chuang. He drove back and forth as straight as a measuring line and wheeled to left and right as neat as a compass-drawn curve. Duke Chuang concluded that even Tsao Fu[9] could do no better, and ordered him to make a hundred circuits and then return to the palace. Yen Ho happened along at the moment and went in to see the duke. "Tung-yeh Chi's horses are going to break down," he said. The duke was silent and gave no answer. In a little while Tung-yeh Chi returned, his

[8] That is, matching up his own innate nature with that of the tree.
[9] Tsao Fu was a famous master of the art of carriage driving. I emend *wen* to *fu*.

horses having in fact broken down. The duke asked Yen Ho, "How did you know that was going to happen?" Yen Ho said, "The strength of the horses was all gone and still he was asking them to go on—that's why I said they would break down."

Artisan Ch'ui could draw as true as a compass or a T square because his fingers changed along with things and he didn't let his mind get in the way. Therefore his Spirit Tower[10] remained unified and unobstructed.

You forget your feet when the shoes are comfortable. You forget your waist when the belt is comfortable. Understanding forgets right and wrong when the mind is comfortable. There is no change in what is inside, no following what is outside, when the adjustment to events is comfortable. You begin with what is comfortable and never experience what is uncomfortable when you know the comfort of forgetting what is comfortable.

A certain Sun Hsiu appeared at the gate of Master Pien Ch'ing-tzu to pay him a call. "When I was living in the village," he said, "no one ever said I lacked good conduct. When I faced difficulty, no one ever said I lacked courage. Yet when I worked the fields, it never seemed to be a good year for crops, and when I served the ruler, it never seemed to be a good time for advancement. So I am an outcast from the villages, an exile from the towns. What crime have I committed against Heaven? Why should I meet this fate?"

Master Pien said, "Have you never heard how the Perfect Man conducts himself? He forgets his liver and gall and thinks no more about his eyes and ears. Vague and aimless, he wan-

---

[10] A Taoist term for the mind.

ders beyond the dirt and dust; free and easy, tending to nothing is his job. This is what is called 'doing but not looking for any thanks, bringing up but not bossing.'[11] Now you show off your wisdom in order to astound the ignorant, work at your good conduct in order to distinguish yourself from the disreputable, going around bright and shining as though you were carrying the sun and moon in your hand! You've managed to keep your body in one piece, you have all the ordinary nine openings, you haven't been struck down midway by blindness or deafness, lameness or deformity—compared to a lot of people, you're a lucky man. How do you have any time to go around complaining against Heaven? Be on your way!"

After Master Sun had left, Master Pien went back into the house, sat down for a while, and then looked up to heaven and sighed. One of his disciples asked, "Why does my teacher sigh?"

Master Pien said, "Just now Sun Hsiu came to see me, and I described to him the virtue of the Perfect Man. I'm afraid he was very startled and may end up in a complete muddle."

"Surely not," said the disciple. "Was what Master Sun said right and what my teacher said wrong? If so, then wrong can certainly never make a muddle out of right. Or was what Master Sun said wrong and what my teacher said right? If so, then he must already have been in a muddle when he came here, so what's the harm?"

"You don't understand," said Master Pien. "Once long ago a bird alighted in the suburbs of the Lu capital. The ruler of Lu was delighted with it, had a T'ai-lao sacrifice prepared for it to feast on, and the Nine Shao music performed for its enjoyment. But the bird immediately began to look unhappy

[11] The same saying is found in the *Tao-te-ching*, secs. 10 and 51.

and dazed, and did not dare to eat or drink. This is what is called trying to nourish a bird with what would nourish you. If you want to nourish a bird with what will nourish a bird, you had best let it roost in the deep forest, float on the rivers and lakes, and live on snakes—then it can feel at ease.[12]

"Now Sun Hsiu is a man of ignorance and little learning. For me to describe to him the virtue of the Perfect Man is like taking a mouse for a ride in a carriage or trying to delight a quail with the music of bells and drums. How could he help but be startled?"

---

[12] The text of the last part of the sentence appears to be corrupt and I make little sense of it. The same anecdote, in somewhat more detailed form, has already appeared on p. 116.

 *EXTERNAL THINGS*

(SECTION 26)

External things cannot be counted on. Hence Lung-feng was executed, Pi Kan was sentenced to death, Prince Chi feigned madness, E Lai was killed, and Chieh and Chou were overthrown.[1] There is no ruler who does not want his ministers to be loyal. But loyal ministers are not always trusted. Hence Wu Yün was thrown into the Yangtze and Ch'ang Hung died in Shu, where the people stored away his blood, and after three years it was transformed into green jade.[2] There is no parent who does not want his son to be filial. But filial sons are not always loved. Hence Hsiao-chi grieved and Tseng Shen sorrowed.[3]

When wood rubs against wood, flames spring up. When metal remains by the side of fire, it melts and flows away.

[1] Kuan Lung-feng, minister to the tyrant Chieh, and Prince Pi Kan, minister to the tyrant Chou, have already appeared on p. 51. Prince Chi was a relative of Chou who had to feign madness in order to escape execution. E Lai assisted Chou and was put to death when Chou was overthrown.

[2] Wu Yün or Wu Tzu-hsü, the loyal minister of Wu, has already appeared on p. 112. He was forced by the king to commit suicide and his body was thrown into the Yangtze. Ch'ang Hung is mentioned in the *Tso chuan* as a minister of the Chou court who was killed in 492 B.C. But, if this is the same man, the story of his exile and suicide in Shu and the miraculous transformation of his blood must come from later legend.

[3] Hsiao-chi was the eminently filial son of King Wu-ting of the Shang; he was said to have been persecuted by an evil stepmother. Tseng Shen, a disciple of Confucius and likewise a paragon of filial piety, was despised by his father.

When the yin and yang go awry, then heaven and earth see astounding sights. Then we hear the crash and roll of thunder, and fire comes in the midst of rain and burns up the great pagoda tree. Delight and sorrow are there to trap man on either side so that he has no escape. Fearful and trembling, he can reach no completion. His mind is as though trussed and suspended between heaven and earth, bewildered and lost in delusion. Profit and loss rub against each other and light the countless fires that burn up the inner harmony of the mass of men. The moon cannot put out the fire, so that in time all is consumed and the Way comes to an end.[4]

Chuang Chou's family was very poor and so he went to borrow some grain from the marquis of Chien-ho. The marquis said, "Why, of course. I'll soon be getting the tribute money from my fief, and when I do, I'll be glad to lend you three hundred pieces of gold. Will that be all right?"

Chuang Chou flushed with anger and said, "As I was coming here yesterday, I heard someone calling me on the road. I turned around and saw that there was a perch in the carriage rut. I said to him, 'Come, perch—what are you doing here?' He replied, 'I am a Wave Official of the Eastern Sea. Couldn't you give me a dipperful of water so I can stay alive?' I said to him, 'Why, of course. I'm just about to start south to visit the kings of Wu and Yüeh. I'll change the course of the West River and send it in your direction. Will that be all right?' The perch flushed with anger and said, 'I've lost

---

[4] This paragraph presents numerous difficulties of interpretation and the translation is tentative at many points. In places the language appears to be that of ancient Chinese medicine, with its theories of the influences of the yin and yang acting within the body. Thus the moon may represent the watery force of the yin, or perhaps the cold light of the mind.

my element! I have nowhere to go! If you can get me a dipper of water, I'll be able to stay alive. But if you give me an answer like that, then you'd best look for me in the dried fish store!' "

Prince Jen made an enormous fishhook with a huge line, baited it with fifty bullocks, settled himself on top of Mount K'uai-chi, and cast with his pole into the eastern sea. Morning after morning he dropped the hook, but for a whole year he got nothing. At last a huge fish swallowed the bait and dived down, dragging the enormous hook. It plunged to the bottom in a fierce charge, rose up and shook its dorsal fins, until the white waves were like mountains and the sea waters lashed and churned. The noise was like that of gods and demons and it spread terror for a thousand li. When Prince Jen had landed his fish, he cut it up and dried it, and from Chih-ho east, from Ts'ang-wu north, there was no one who did not get his fill. Since then the men of later generations who have piddling talents and a penchant for odd stories all astound each other by repeating the tale.

Now if you shoulder your pole and line, march to the ditches and gullies, and watch for minnows and perch, then you'll have a hard time ever landing a big fish. If you parade your little theories and fish for the post of district magistrate, you will be far from the Great Understanding. So if a man has never heard of the style of Prince Jen, he's a long way from being able to join with the men who run the world.

The Confucians rob graves in accordance with the *Odes* and ritual. The big Confucian announces to his underlings: "The east grows light! How is the matter proceeding?"

The little Confucians say: "We haven't got the graveclothes off him yet but there's a pearl in his mouth![5] Just as the Ode says:

> Green, green the grain
> Growing on grave mound slopes;
> If in life you gave no alms
> In death how do you deserve a pearl?"

They push back his sidelocks, press down his beard, and then one of them pries into his chin with a little metal gimlet and gently pulls apart the jaws so as not to injure the pearl in his mouth.

A disciple of Lao Lai-tzu[6] was out gathering firewood when he happened to meet Confucius. He returned and reported, "There's a man over there with a long body and short legs, his back a little humped and his ears set way back, who looks as though he were trying to attend to everything within the four seas. I don't know who it can be."

Lao Lai-tzu said, "That's K'ung Ch'iu. Tell him to come over here!"

When Confucius arrived, Lao Lai-tzu said, "Ch'iu, get rid of your proud bearing and that knowing look on your face and you can become a gentleman!"

Confucius bowed and stepped back a little, a startled and changed expression on his face, and then asked, "Do you think I can make any progress in my labors?"

Lao Lai-tzu said, "You can't bear to watch the sufferings of

[5] The pearl or other precious stone customarily placed in the mouth of the corpse at burial.
[6] A Taoist sage and reputed author of a work in sixteen sections which is no longer extant. He is sometimes identified with Lao Tzu.

one age, and so you go and make trouble for ten thousand ages to come![7] Are you just naturally a boor? Or don't you have the sense to understand the situation? You take pride in practicing charity and making people happy[8]—the shame of it will follow you all your days! These are the actions, the 'progress' of mediocre men—men who pull each other around with fame, drag each other into secret schemes, join together to praise Yao and condemn Chieh, when the best thing would be to forget them both and put a stop to praise! What is contrary cannot fail to be injured, what moves [when it shouldn't] cannot fail to be wrong. The sage is hesitant and reluctant to begin an affair, and so he always ends in success. But what good are these actions of yours? They end in nothing but a boast!"[9]

Lord Yüan of Sung one night dreamed he saw a man with disheveled hair who peered in at the side door of his chamber and said, "I come from the Tsai-lu Deeps. I was on my way as envoy from the Clear Yangtze to the court of the Lord of the Yellow River when a fisherman named Yü Chü caught me!"

When Lord Yüan woke up, he ordered his men to divine the meaning, and they replied, "This is a sacred turtle." "Is there a fisherman named Yü Chü?" he asked, and his attendants replied, "There is." "Order Yü Chü to come to court!" he said.

The next day Yü Chü appeared at court and the ruler said, "What kind of fish have you caught recently?"

[7] Following texts which read *wu* in place of *ao*.
[8] The meaning is very doubtful.
[9] This last speech of Lao Lai-tzu presents numerous difficulties and the translation is tentative.

Yü Chü replied, "I caught a white turtle in my net. It's five feet around."

"Present your turtle!" ordered the ruler. When the turtle was brought, the ruler could not decide whether to kill it or let it live and, being in doubt, he consulted his diviners, who replied, "Kill the turtle and divine with it—it will bring good luck." Accordingly the turtle was stripped of its shell, and of seventy-two holes drilled in it for prognostication, not one failed to yield a true answer.[10]

Confucius said, "The sacred turtle could appear to Lord Yüan in a dream but it couldn't escape from Yü Chü's net. It knew enough to give correct answers to seventy-two queries but it couldn't escape the disaster of having its belly ripped open. So it is that knowledge has its limitations, and the sacred has that which it can do nothing about. Even the most perfect wisdom can be outwitted by ten thousand schemers. Fish do not [know enough to] fear a net, but only to fear pelicans. Discard little wisdom and great wisdom will become clear. Discard goodness and goodness will come of itself. The little child learns to speak, though it has no learned teachers —because it lives with those who know how to speak."

Hui Tzu said to Chuang Tzu, "Your words are useless!"

Chuang Tzu said, "A man has to understand the useless before you can talk to him about the useful. The earth is certainly vast and broad, though a man uses no more of it than the area he puts his feet on. If, however, you were to dig away all the earth from around his feet until you reached

[10] Small indentations were drilled in the carapace and heat was applied: divination was based on the shape of the cracks which resulted.

the Yellow Springs,[11] then would the man still be able to make use of it?"

"No, it would be useless," said Hui Tzu.

"It is obvious, then," said Chuang Tzu, "that the useless has its use."

Chuang Tzu said, "If you have the capacity to wander, how can you keep from wandering? But if you do not have the capacity to wander, how can you wander? A will that takes refuge in conformity, behavior that is aloof and eccentric—neither of these, alas, is compatible with perfect wisdom and solid virtue. You stumble and fall but fail to turn back; you race on like fire and do not look behind you. But though you may be one time a ruler, another time a subject, this is merely a matter of the times. Such distinctions change with the age and you cannot call either one or the other lowly. Therefore I say, the Perfect Man is never a stickler in his actions.

"To admire antiquity and despise the present—this is the fashion of scholars. And if one is to look at the present age after the fashion of Hsi-wei, then who can be without prejudice?[12] Only the Perfect Man can wander in the world

---

[11] See above, p. 108, n. 17.

[12] Hsi-wei, identified as a mythical ruler of high antiquity, has already appeared above, p. 77, as the sage who "held up heaven and earth." The Confucians and Mo-ists are the most notorious extollers of antiquity, but the same tendency is discernible at times in the Taoist school, e.g., in Lao Tzu's description of the ideal simplicity and primitiveness of the society of very ancient times. I suspect that "the fashion of Hsi-wei" is a reference to these advocates of ancient simplicity within the Taoist school, though our understanding of the passage is greatly hampered by the fact that we know almost nothing about the Hsi-wei legend. As this passage makes clear, Chuang Tzu's ideal "wandering"—i.e., living in accordance with the Way —does not permit either a forced conformity with the world or a forced withdrawal from, and denial of, the world.

without taking sides, can follow along with men without losing himself. His teachings are not to be learned, and one who understands his meaning has no need for him.[13]

"The eye that is penetrating sees clearly, the ear that is penetrating hears clearly, the nose that is penetrating distinguishes odors, the mouth that is penetrating distinguishes flavors, the mind that is penetrating has understanding, and the understanding that is penetrating has virtue. In all things, the Way does not want to be obstructed, for if there is obstruction, there is choking; if the choking does not cease, there is disorder; and disorder harms the life of all creatures.

"All things that have consciousness depend upon breath. But if they do not get their fill of breath, it is not the fault of Heaven. Heaven opens up the passages and supplies them day and night without stop. But man on the contrary blocks up the holes. The cavity of the body is a many-storied vault; the mind has its Heavenly wanderings. But if the chambers are not large and roomy, then the wife and mother-in-law will fall to quarreling. If the mind does not have its Heavenly wanderings, then the six apertures of sensation will defeat each other.

"The great forests, the hills and mountains excel man in the fact that their growth is irrepressible. [In man] virtue spills over into a concern for fame, and a concern for fame spills over into a love of show. Schemes are laid in time of crisis; wisdom is born from contention; obstinacy comes from sticking to a position; government affairs are arranged for the convenience of the mob.[14] In spring, when the seasonable rains and sunshine come, the grass and trees spring to life,

---

[13] The second part of the sentence is obscure in the original.

[14] I take fame, show, schemes, wisdom, and the arranging of government affairs for the convenience of the mob to be "unnatural" and undesirable aims and activities that interfere with man's growth.

and the sickles and hoes are for the first time prepared for use. At that time, over half the grass and trees that had been pushed over begin to grow again, though no one knows why.[15]

"Stillness and silence can benefit the ailing, massage can give relief to the aged, and rest and quiet can put a stop to agitation. But these are remedies which the troubled and weary man has recourse to. The man who is at ease does not need them and has never bothered to ask about them. The Holy Man does not bother to ask what methods the sage uses to reform the world. The sage does not bother to ask what methods the worthy man uses to reform the age. The worthy man does not bother to ask what methods the gentleman uses to reform the state. The gentleman does not bother to ask what methods the petty man uses to get along with the times.

"There was a man of Yen Gate who, on the death of his parents, won praise by starving and disfiguring himself, and was rewarded with the post of Official Teacher. The other people of the village likewise starved and disfigured themselves, and over half of them died. Yao offered the empire to Hsü Yu and Hsü Yu fled from him. T'ang offered it to Wu Kuang and Wu Kuang railed at him. When Chi T'o heard of this, he took his disciples and went off to sit by the K'uan River, where the feudal lords went to console him for three years. Shen-t'u Ti for the same reason jumped into the Yellow River.[16]

[15] This whole paragraph, and especially the last sentence, is very difficult to interpret, and there is no agreement among commentators as to the exact meaning.

[16] Hsü Yu, the recluse who refused Yao's throne, has appeared above, on p. 26. A similar story is told of King T'ang and the recluse Wu Kuang. Chi T'o and Shen-t'u Ti, along with Hsü Yu and Wu Kuang, have been mentioned above, p. 75, but we know nothing of their stories. Apparently they withdrew or committed suicide out of sympathy for the insult which had been done to Wu Kuang in offering him a throne.

"The fish trap exists because of the fish; once you've gotten the fish, you can forget the trap. The rabbit snare exists because of the rabbit; once you've gotten the rabbit, you can forget the snare. Words exist because of meaning; once you've gotten the meaning, you can forget the words. Where can I find a man who has forgotten words so I can have a word with him?"

INDEX

OTHER WORKS IN THE COLUMBIA ASIAN STUDIES SERIES

Translations from the Asian Classics

7. *Iqbal: Poet-Philosopher of Pakistan*, ed. Hafeez Malik   1971

8. *The Golden Tradition: An Anthology of Urdu Poetry*, ed. and tr. Ahmed Ali. Also in paperback ed.   1973

9. *Conquerors and Confucians: Aspects of Political Change in Late Yūan China*, by John W. Dardess   1973

10. *The Unfolding of Neo-Confucianism*, by Wm. Theodore de Bary and the Conference on Seventeenth-Century Chinese Thought. Also in paperback ed.   1975

11. *To Acquire Wisdom: The Way of Wang Yang-ming*, by Julia Ching   1976

12. *Gods, Priests, and Warriors: The Bhṛgus of the Mahābhārata*, by Robert P. Goldman   1977

13. *Mei Yao-ch'en and the Development of Early Sung Poetry*, by Jonathan Chaves   1976

14. *The Legend of Semimaru, Blind Musician of Japan*, by Susan Matisoff   1977

15. *Sir Sayyid Ahmad Khan and Muslim Modernization in India and Pakistan*, by Hafeez Malik   1980

16. *The Khilafat Movement: Religious Symbolism and Political Mobilization in India*, by Gail Minault   1982

17. *The World of K'ung Shang-jen: A Man of Letters in Early Ch'ing China*, by Richard Strassberg   1983

18. *The Lotus Boat: The Origins of Chinese Tz'u Poetry in T'ang Popular Culture*, by arsha L. Wagner   1984

Companions to Asian Studies

An Introduction to Chinese Civilization, ed.
  John Meskill, with the assistance of
  J. Mason Gentzler   1973
An Introduction to Japanese Civilization, ed.
  Arthur E. Tiedemann   1974
Ukifune: Love in the Tale of Genji, ed. Andrew
  Pekarik   1982
The Pleasures of Japanese Literature, by Donald
  Keene   1988
A Guide to Oriental Classics, eds. Wm.
  Theodore de Bary and Ainslie T. Embree;
  3d edition ed. Amy Vladeck Heinrich, 2 vols.   1989

Introduction to Asian Civilizations

Wm. Theodore de Bary, Editor

Sources of Japanese Tradition, 1958; paperback
  ed., 2 vols., 1964
Sources of Indian Tradition, 1958; paperback
  ed., 2 vols., 1964; 2d ed., 2 vols., 1988
Sources of Chinese Tradition, 1960;
  paperback ed., 2 vols., 1964

Neo-Confucian Studies

*Instructions for Practical Living and Other Neo-
  Confucian Writings by Wang Yang-ming*, tr.
  Wing-tsit Chan   1963
*Reflections on Things at Hand: The Neo-Confucian
  Anthology*, comp. Chu Hsi and Lü
  Tsu-ch'ien, tr. Wing-tsit Chan   1967